JELLY

WITH BOMPAS & PARR

PHOTOGRAPHY BY CHRIS TERRY

PAVILION

First published in the United Kingdom in 2010 by
PAVILION BOOKS
10 Southcombe Street, London W14 0RA

An imprint of Anova Books Company Ltd

Commissioning Editor: Emily Preece-Morrison
Designer: Georgina Hewitt
Photographer: Chris Terry
Prop Stylist: Wei Tang
Copy Editor: Caroline Curtis
Americaniser: Constance Novis
Production: Oliver Jeffreys
Index: Patricia Hymans

ISBN: 978-1-86205-879-8

A CIP catalogue record for this book is available from the British Library.

10 9 8 7 6 5 4 3 2

Reproduction by Rival Colour Limited, UK
Printed and bound by 1010 Printing International Ltd, China

www.anovabooks.com

WHAT PEOPLE ARE SAYING ABOUT BOMPAS & PARR:

"Not since Heston Blumenthal burst on the scene has anyone brought such crazed ambition to food design." THE TELEGRAPH

"I think Bompas and Parr are geniuses. It's the principles of rock'n'roll applied to food." ALEX JAMES, MUSICIAN AND COLUMNIST

"Culinary deviants." THE GUARDIAN

"Like Gilbert and George, Bompas and Parr always seem to pop up together, often wearing cool oversized spectacles or ostentatiously fogeyish bow-ties." THE TELEGRAPH

"Willy Wonka during his freewheeling student days." THE INDEPENDENT

"England's leading jelly artists, or as they call themselves, jellymongers." NEW YORK TIMES

"If you're going to do silly, do it in style." THE TIMES

Named by THE INDEPENDENT as one of "the 15 people who will define the future of arts in Britain."

CONTENTS

INTRODUCTION

"When the going gets weird, the weird turn pro."

HUNTER S. THOMPSON

The life of a jellymonger is wobbly, largely ridiculous and often downright weird. If it's not strange enough explaining to people what a *jellymonger* is, it's even stranger describing what else we do with food and how we really do make a living selling jelly.

The jelly business started when we tried to set up a stall at Borough Market in the summer of 2007. They weren't interested but we managed to pull in a couple of jobs making fresh fruit jellies for parties. No one was making jelly, so there was an obvious gap in the market. Our inspiration came from two sources: childhood nostalgia and the knowledge that England used to be famous in the culinary world for two things – jelly and roasting. Jelly had somehow taken a serious tumble in the nation's affections. After the *Sunday Times* included us in an article about the renaissance of traditional English food, business took off dramatically.

If you think that jelly starts and ends with the lurid stuff you get at children's parties, then you've got a lot to learn. Jelly has a long, illustrious history, and much of it seems unbelievable: we didn't know what we were getting ourselves into until we started studying old cookery books. Jelly used to be one of the noblest things you could eat at a meal. Forget making jelly with champagne: jelly used to be made with gold. Even Henry VIII was a fan, requesting it to grace his banqueting tables on state occasions. Victorian England was jelly's heyday: embarrassed French chefs even came on secret pilgrimages across the channel to get jelly tips and pick up exquisite moulds.

We are working hard to restore jelly to its culinary throne. With this book, we've been given the opportunity to tell you everything we know about it. The best thing about jelly is that, with decent instructions, it's really easy to make and the results are spectacular. Jelly is magical: it has the ability to make people laugh hysterically, is loaded with nostalgia and, best of all, can taste wild. OK, we're not giving a sermon here, but you get the idea: jelly rocks.

When you start making and serving proper jelly, we hope that your views on food will change. People love jelly: it's one of the only foods to be guaranteed

Above

Our first jelly commission – the Innocent village fête in 2007.

a reaction of some sort. The reaction we get has made us reassess what food is really about. Jelly generates so much excitement that we wondered how we could approach other types of food to elicit similar reactions.

Bompas & Parr has always been about creating culinary projects that explode people's pre-conceived notions of food. Whether it's assaulting people's senses with scratch 'n' sniff cards at food films or creating walk-in clouds of gin and tonic, we've found there's no limit to what you can do with food. The same is true for jelly: by the time you've finished reading this book, you'll see that there's a whole lot more to jelly than you may have thought. And I'll bet we'll still be coming up with new things to do with jelly many years from now.

Neither of us trained to be chefs. The weird thing is, Sam would probably be a politician by now if he hadn't got into jelly whereas Harry trained for six years to become an architect but left it all for jelly. Bizarrely it was Harry's professor who suggested that there was a lot of mileage in jelly: maybe he was trying to say something about Harry's architectural prowess. So, with no formal culinary training, our approach to cooking is vastly different to most people's in the food industry.

As the business progressed, we really needed to get a grip on making our own moulds. Those beautiful copper Victorian moulds are extortionately expensive,

Barajas 'Jelly' Airport
Rogers Stirk Harbour + Partners

and with no moulds we didn't have a hope of doing anything decent with jelly. So, never shy of a challenge, we gave ourselves a huge headache: we invited architects to design jellies in the shape of their buildings and offered to make the moulds for them. We called it the Architectural Jelly Design Competition and we did it to benefit disaster relief charity Article 25. We then planned a jelly banquet, to be held in the stunning portico of University College London. We were all set to kick-start a jelly comeback.

The jelly banquet became one of 2008's stories of the summer (see also p.150). It was big news: everyone was going jelly crazy. It was helped by securing the support of some of the biggest names in architecture, including Lord Foster and Rogers Stirk Harbour + Partners. Foster designed a jelly in homage to his 'wobbly' millennium bridge, and Rogers created the genius Barajas 'jelly' airport – a striking multi-flavoured modular jelly. Sam even ended up taking jellies on BBC Radio 4's 'Today' programme.

The impending banquet forced us to work out how to make jelly moulds. Using the same programs that architects use to design buildings, we're able to model the jelly and then translate it to a physical model, using a process called 3D printing. The 3D printer prints glue onto a moving bed of plaster, allowing a model of the jelly to be created. The resulting form can then be vacuum-formed with plastic to create a functional mould. Of course it's not as simple as it sounds, and we are still perfecting the technique.

We had over one hundred entries into the competition and we assembled a panel of design and food experts to judge them in terms of innovation, aesthetics and, most importantly, 'wobble-factor'. Professor Stephen Gage, from University College London and one of the judges of the competition, summed up the architectural appeal of jelly like this:

> *"As babies, we first learn about our world by touching it and putting bits of it in our mouth. Part of our subconscious appreciation of shape may well be a dim memory of how it might feel in our mouth. Thus a dome is round and coolly satisfying, while a pointed building is like a sharp and dangerous knife. Jelly architecture returns architecture to the mouth, where we can once again taste it."*

Above and Opposite

Entries from the Architectural Jelly Design Competition. Above left: Wobbly Bridge by Lord Foster;
Above right: Wheatgrass Jelly by Atkins Global; Opposite: Barajas Jelly Airport by Rogers Stirk Harbour + Partners.

Well, that's enough theory for now. We had over 2000 people due to attend the banquet, and we knew that we would have to do something extraordinary to keep them all entertained. Although jellies are striking, it's hard to make them very big. So for the jellies we made a table 14m (46ft) long, which held hundreds of individually illuminated jellies, and was driven by an ingenious 'waggle engine' that made everything wobble. To set it all off, we commissioned a jelly ballet to be performed on the steps of the portico. Harry made giant plastic spoons for the dancers to use to interpret the music.

The night really started to get under way when Heston Blumenthal, who had been at the banquet getting inspiration for his own TV series 'Feast', agreed to hand out the prize to the winning architect. At this point, the crowd started shouting 'fight, fight, fight', drowning him out until two brave pioneers dived into a pool full of jelly and started wrestling. It was a great jelly moment.

Later in the evening, as the clock struck 11pm, a jelly in the shape of St Paul's Cathedral was hurled out of the portico and onto the crowd below. Within seconds, a huge food fight broke out. It was something that we weren't expecting, but it was brilliant fun.

Above and opposite

Opposite: Jelly St Paul's Cathedral, designed by Bompas & Parr.

Above: Harry and Sam at Alcoholic Architecture, their gin cloud installation.

Jelly and alcohol go hand in hand. Those jellies that Henry VIII served were alcoholic, and throughout history alcohol has often been added to jelly. To see how far we could really push alcohol consumption, we created Alcoholic Architecture, a bar where people could literally walk into a cloud of vaporized gin and tonic. The alcoholic fog was a global hit, although we suspect that it will be outlawed if we ever try to repeat it: some things are best left as memories (see also p.152).

More child-friendly was working with Jell-O, who gave us the opportunity to build some wonderfully ambitious jelly sculptures. We even created a vast jelly map of America for an edition of the 'Early Show' on CBS. Although it took months of work to design and make the moulds, the hardest part was getting up at 3 a.m. to unmould all the individual jellies that made up the map.

Our approach to food has been influenced heavily by creating culinary events and then observing how people react to what's around them. Food is a really complicated subject. We have to eat to survive, yet what we put in our mouths is loaded with so much meaning that it's easy to forget this. Sure, we both like good food, but good food comes in many forms: a packet of cheeseburger flavour crisps is just as incredible as anything that you would eat at a Michelin starred restaurant. And with jelly, high and low cultures really do get slammed together. For example, the technology we use to design and make jelly moulds is of the moment, yet that same mould can be filled with organic fruit or with artificially flavoured packet jelly. The truth is that by the time you unmould and present the jelly, the original ingredients are only a very small part of people's experience.

Food should be, above all else, enjoyable. Next time you're invited to a dinner party, don't bring trendy bijou chocolates. Instead bring Ferrero Rocher – but arrange them on a silver tray in a pyramid. It's cheaper, more fun and, unless you're a chocolate fascist, probably as tasty. It's all too easy to have food prejudice, but it is worth thinking for a moment about why things are as they are. For example, don't forget that there are far more chemicals in the kitchen of El Bulli than there are in any burger.

In a world where food is becoming so worthy, it's time to rediscover the joy that can come from cooking. Jelly is as good a place as any to start enjoying food. So, whether you make jellies with foraged fruit or with juice from the supermarket, you'll still have fun. And fun should, for once, be important.

Above

The wobble that woos: jellying in America.

A BRIEF HISTORY OF JELLY

Jelly has quite some history: it's been around in one form or another for thousands of years. The origins of jelly are somewhat shrouded in mystery, though one thing is clear: if you boil any meat or fish and let the stock cool then, guess what, you've got jelly. OK, so it's more like pork pie jelly than raspberry jelly but, like it or not, the basis of both is the same. And hundreds of years ago people realized that the jelly they could make from boiling meat had a lot of potential.

Out of curiosity, we decided that we needed to get medieval and make jelly from scratch; there's no point calling yourself a jellymonger if you can't take flesh and turn it into pudding. We found that by taking a pig's worth of trotters and boiling them up, you can indeed make a passable jelly. As long as you don't eat it that is, because the downside is that it tastes pretty porkie. If Jell-O sold pig flavour jelly, we don't imagine it would fly off the shelves – although we do admire Marks and Spencer for *Percy Pig*; a gelatine-based sweet shaped as a friendly pig is warped genius.

Unsurprisingly, some of the earliest known jelly recipes were for savoury jellies. Take Taillevent, head cook to Charles V, who in 1381 gives a recipe for a 'jelly of slimy fish, and of meat'. Sounds disgusting, but apparently it turned out OK. And, even then, clarity and a clean flavour were important to jellies: it's not many recipes that include the line 'If you wish to make jelly, you do not need to sleep.' Making a decent jelly involved lots of clarifying of the stock using egg whites, and lots of straining through expensive jelly cloths. Making jelly took time. And time means money – so serving a jelly was an impressive, and generous, act. When the soon-to-be King Henry IV was travelling back from a pilgrimage to the Holy Lands in 1393, he authorized his cook to travel to Venice to buy 3 yards of fabric for making jelly cloths. That's some jelly emergency he was having.

In medieval Britain, it wasn't unusual to have sweet and savoury flavours combined; sugar was rare and so it was used like a spice, added to almost anything. Take mince pies; they were traditionally meat-based, containing more ground mutton than the usual bits and pieces. And, by the way, they taste amazing – the meat loosens the texture, making them much lighter. So perhaps jelly did always taste a little meaty and people were used to it.

Above

Sam and Harry get Victorian with their meaty desserts.

In the late medieval period, fasting was the name of the game: for many days in the Church calendar, fish had to be eaten instead of meat. Forty consecutive days eating fish during Lent was enough to deaden everyone's palates. For the poor, Lent meant forty days of salted fish. And for the rich few, jelly provided the variety and amusement. It's at this point that the records start to refer to jelly moulds. Fish-shaped jellies made with sweet almond milk were popular, as was the strange practice of making replica jelly eggs.

By the sixteenth century, jelly was becoming more refined as a dish in its own right. Cooks had discovered that a variety of gelling agents could be used for setting jellies. These included calves feet and the curious isinglass, which is made from the swim-bladders of sturgeon. The addition of sugar produced jellies more recognizable to the modern palate. Jelly was the preserve of the rich and was used liberally as a form of conspicuous consumption. At this time, sugar was wildly expensive, and kept under lock and key by the mistress of the house. Making sweetened jellies was an easy way to demonstrate the household's wealth.

Colour too became a priority. We were relieved to see that old recipes often suggest making striped jelly by making a batch of jelly and then splitting it into parts and colouring them differently. Often, when we are making jellies that are going to be used for photoshoots, this is exactly what we do. Cooks once used almond milk to turn jellies white; we just use milk. And forget using saffron to turn a jelly yellow; Dr. Oetker does a great line in food colouring. At this point, the cook's art lay in making something that looked like a jelly rather than making something that we would call authentic: a red jelly did not signify that it would taste of strawberries.

The separation of savoury and sweet was made complete by the development of the banquet. We think of a 'banquet' as a feast, but the term was originally used to describe the new course that developed during the Renaissance: a sweet final course, served to round off the meal. In England, this course even had its own architecture: the banqueting house. These were ornate follies built solely for creating a showcase for sugary desserts. It's no surprise to learn that Harry is particularly keen on building one.

One important dish on the banquet table was *leche*: a sweet milk jelly perfumed with rosewater. The jelly was cut into squares and one half was gilded to create an impressive chequerboard effect. This combination of jelly and gold laid the foundations for the elaborate suspensions of gold leaf in Victorian jellies. For Sam, it has also laid the foundations of an extremely expensive addiction.

Early banqueting tables had elaborate sugar sculptures and moulded marzipan pastes, formed into interesting shapes using hand-carved wooden moulds. It wasn't long before a whole industry developed around making moulds. The first jelly moulds were carved from sycamore wood and were used to make flummery, which evolved into the modern blancmange. A century later, complex copper moulds allowed cooks to experiment with such culinary witticisms as full-colour replicas of bacon and eggs.

The golden age of jelly dawned at the start of the eighteenth century. Jelly-glasses were developed to show off multi-coloured jellies in their full splendour, and from the mid-eighteenth century the Staffordshire potteries began producing some of the earliest ceramic moulds, made from salt-glazed stoneware. These moulds are surprisingly shallow and incredibly fragile. Food historian Ivan Day kindly showed us how to use them – although it was somewhat nerve-racking. We made blancmange fish and then gilded them.

Ivan also showed us a very rare obelisk creamware mould made by Neale and Son in about 1790. These moulds are incredible – they were specifically developed to make jellies for decoration rather than eating. The mould comes in two parts: an outer shell and an ornately decorated internal core with a base. You pour jelly into the gap between the outer mould and the core. Then you remove the outer mould, leaving a thin layer of jelly cladding the decorated core. The idea is that the gentle scalloped edges of the jelly would catch the flickering candlelight and animate the fauna painted on the core. Ivan had only recently bought one of these moulds at vast expense and he was keen to give it a go – especially since every other example was in a museum case. In practice, these moulds are really hard to use but they illustrate that jelly really did signify good taste.

The fashion for jellies was a boomtime for the more adventurous entrepreneur. We like to think that we coined the word jellymonger, but in eighteenth century Manchester, Elizabeth Raffald was making money selling, among other things, 'Globe Jellies'. The concept was simple – using a large bowl, clear jellies could be set to make a huge convex lens. Her innovations, however, were anything but simple: she suggested fanciful creations of clear fish-ponds with white or gold flummery fish set on the bottom; the contents of whole fruit-baskets arranged in jelly; and a jelly planetarium of milky-white flummery moons and stars set against a black night sky.

Then came the Victorian era, when jelly reached its pinnacle. Copper moulds were more complex than ever, and had the advantage of being excellent conductors, allowing the jelly to be removed easily with just a dip in warm water. Hollow inserts were developed for moulds such as the Alexandra Cross. A cross-shaped insert was placed inside the main body of red jelly as it set. When solid, the insert was filled with warm water, then demoulded, and the cavity filled with a white jelly. Presented and cut horizontally, the jelly emerged as slices bearing the Danish flag. They even had special knives for cutting jellies.

Above

Advert for our hero Mrs. Marshall's line of gelatine.

Above and Overleaf

Above: Here Mrs. Marshall flogs her own-brand moulds.

Overleaf: A spread for a single diner at the Victorian Breakfast we created

at Warwick castle. For full details see p.149.

Mrs. Marshall, owner of Marshall's Cookery School, combined a fine line in jellies with an even finer line in marketing. Her books are exercises in self-promotion; recipes for Alexandra jelly are shamelessly supplemented by a catalogue of her own-brand moulds. And she insisted that her readers use her own-brand leaf gelatine; her advertisements warn against the lesser-quality imitations of her competitors. Which allows us to suggest that going to www.jellymongers.co.uk is a great place to start any mould collection.

The widespread popularity of jelly, combined with advances in food processing technology, led to the first preparations of 'table jellies' by companies such as Rowntree's and Hartley's in the U.K. In 1881, Rowntree's started the first domestic production of fruit pastilles, which had previously been the preserve of the French. This success, coupled with some studious forays into artificial flavouring and gelling, led to the production of Rowntree's Table Jellies in 1901.

The story of Rowntree's and Hartley's is remarkably similar: two companies headed by entrepreneurial grocers, which rose to dominate the market. The Hartley's factory at Aintree was the centre of a village dedicated to producing jams and jellies. Each year, the town's residents stopped other work to pick a bumper crop of fruit, which was then transformed into jelly cubes. The easily recognizable jelly cube is unique to the U.K. – the rest of Europe and the United States use powdered gelatine.

Powdered gelatine was first patented in the United States in 1845, but was not widely used. Then, at the beginning of the twentieth century, fruit syrups were added to the gelatine, and a product called Jell-O was born. It soon became a must-have pudding on every table. Recently, we were commisioned by Jell-O to create a whole series of moulds for a media tour of the United States. It was a lot of fun, even if we weren't allowed to sell directly to kids (unlike Bill Cosby, the face of Jell-O for decades).

By the 1950s, jellies became more popular then ever; jellies are quick to make, and the new refrigerators meant that their setting times were drastically reduced. Furthermore, jelly had come to be seen as a healthy alternative dessert: so much so that in the 1950s *Vogue* published an article on the newest fad for the jelly diet, pitting one wobble against another.

As jelly became increasingly easy and cheap to make, it led to a rapid decline in the craft of making jelly moulds. By the start of World War II, the jelly mould industry in England had effectively ceased. Plastic moulds helped to replace part of the void that was left, but the figurative designs hardly reflect jelly's fine pedigree.

At Bompas and Parr we're changing all that. We've made moulds of everything, from nuclear submarines to skyscrapers. Making our own moulds allows us to explore jelly's heritage and to push the boundaries of the medium. And we're not the only ones who have rediscovered jelly: innovative chefs are constantly delivering new flavours and textures. Jelly has endless possibilities.

THE UNIVERSAL
JELLY PRINCIPLE

If stable food is not your thing, you should be pleased to hear that almost anything can be turned into a jelly. With a distinctly misguided spirit of adventure, we once created an entire Christmas dinner in one tall and very wobbly striped jelly. There were layers of sprouts, parsnips, potatoes, stuffing, bread sauce and, of course, turkey consommé studded with artfully positioned mini sausages and bacon rashers. Once you can master this jelly Everest – it had jelly foothills made of champagne, burgundy, port and sherry – you're qualified to jelly anything. At least, we like to think so.

To make a jelly, whether it's sweet or savoury, you need to combine two components: a liquid and gelatine. At its most basic, the jelly recipe can be turned into a sum:

$$\textit{Liquid} + \textit{Gelling Agent} = \textit{Jelly}$$

This principle will be expanded upon and explained in the next section. And by the time you are done reading it, you will be able to turn any liquid into a jelly.

Turn to the next page for a step-by-step guide to basic jelly making.

STEP ONE: CHOOSE YOUR MOULD

First fill your mould with water and pour this water back into a measuring jug. Knowing the volume of liquid that you need to fill your mould allows you to calculate how much gelatine you will need. To get you started, here's a good rule of thumb:

> *1 leaf of gelatine sets 100ml/3 ½fl oz of liquid*

How simple is that! If you are setting the jelly in a glass and not planning on ummoulding it, use less gelatine – see the table below for guidance. Use either platinum or gold leaf gelatine: it's readily available in supermarkets. Powdered gelatine is actually harder to use and the results are not as good. Using scissors, cut up each leaf of gelatine into about six pieces and put them in a heatproof bowl. Use a measuring jug to mix up the required volume of liquid. This could be anything: fruit juice, wine, even Irn Bru. There are plenty of recipes in the next chapter to get you started. Next, pour some of this liquid over the gelatine so it is just covered. Leave to one side for at least 10 minutes, or until the gelatine has softened.

Mould volume	Unmoulding jelly	Not unmoulding jelly
300ml/10fl oz	3 leaves gelatine	2.2 leaves gelatine
400ml/14fl oz	4	2.9
500ml/18fl oz	5	3.6
600ml/1 pint	6	4.3
700ml/1¼ pints	7	5
800ml/28fl oz	8	5.7
900ml/1½ pints	9	6.4
1 litre/1¾ pints	10	7.1

STEP TWO:
MELTING THE GELATINE

Put some hot water in a small pan and bring it up to a slow simmer. Then place the bowl of softened gelatine on top. Stir from time to time until the gelatine has dissolved. This should take about 10 minutes, but it can take longer if you are using milk as the liquid.

STEP THREE:
COMBINING THE GELATINE WITH THE MIXTURE

Add the remaining liquid to the bowl of melted gelatine and give it a good stir. Then pour the contents of the bowl through a sieve and back into the measuring jug. The sieve will catch any small lumps of undissolved gelatine, and if you were using lemon juice it will catch the pips.

Now slowly pour the unset jelly into your mould. If there are any air bubbles on the surface, skim them off using a teaspoon. Otherwise, they will still be there when the jelly has set. Place the jelly in the refrigerator, and about 6 hours later it will be set and ready for unmoulding.

STEP FOUR:
UNMOULDING

Jellies come to life when they are unmoulded. The unmoulding process is theoretically straightforward: put the jelly mould into a basin of warm water until a little of the jelly around the edge has melted and then turn it out onto a plate.

It sounds easy, but there's real skill in judging the time the mould needs to be submerged in the warm water. Sometimes you must be patient; on other occasions, it will unmould in a flash. Depending on the thickness of the metal or plastic and the temperature of the water, it can take between two seconds and 30 seconds for the jelly to release.

When you unmould directly onto a plate, the jelly will stick to the surface wherever it lands. To prevent this, wet the plate before turning out the jelly. This allows you to reposition the jelly to the plate's centre. If you've got this far, you're almost a jelly pro. Good work! If you are serving jelly for a dinner party, you can unmould it in advance and leave it on its plate in the refrigerator, where it will keep quite happily for several hours.

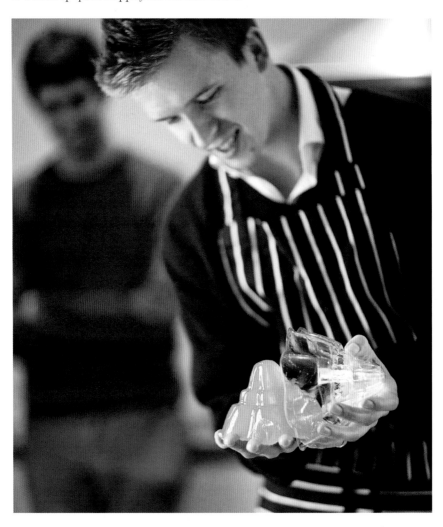

Sugar syrup

Jelly straight from the refrigerator will be thoroughly chilled. Remember that the flavour of anything cold is less obvious than something at room temperature. So when making jellies, the liquid you use must be slightly sweeter than you want it finally to taste.

The best way of adding sugar to a juice is to use sugar syrup, which dilutes and sweetens the fruit juice at the same time. It's a good idea to dilute fruit juice down before making it into a jelly; otherwise, it will be more like jam.

If you want total control over the sweetness of any jelly in this book, use sugar syrup and omit any other sugar from the recipe. And use a combination of syrup and water to make up the volume of the fruit juice you're using.

Making sugar syrup is very easy and if you have some leftover, it's got plenty of other uses. It's the best way to get sweetness into cocktails. By the same token it's handy for making iced coffee in the summer. You can also use the syrup as the base for poaching fruit and adding sweetness to fruit salads.

Bring the water to the boil in a saucepan and take it off the heat. Then stir in the sugar until it has dissolved. Easy!

Of course, if you don't think you will need this much syrup just adjust the volume of water and weight of sugar proportionately at a ratio of 1:1 (1ml water to 1g sugar).

If you have leftover syrup, it can be stored covered in the refrigerator for up to 2 weeks.

MAKES 1KG/2LB 4OZ
(ABOUT 750ML/1⅓ PINTS)

500ML/18FL OZ WATER

500G/1LB 2OZ CASTER OR
GRANULATED SUGAR

FREQUENTLY ASKED QUESTIONS:

What type of gelatine should I use and why?

Always use leaf gelatine. Leaf gelatine creates jellies with the smoothest texture and is cleaner tasting than powdered gelatine. Gelatine is graded Olympic medal style – but jelly is more fun than sport, so there is also a top-notch platinum grade. Use either platinum or gold grade: anything else, and you're jellies will be more Eddie the Eagle than Usain Bolt. Luckily, most supermarkets will take your money in return for a pack of their finest gold or platinum grades. The higher up the medal table your gelatine is, the purer it will be, with corresponding improvements in clarity, taste and gelling strength.

But the packet says I should use a specific amount of gelatine.

This is where the dark art of jellying comes in. Don't be fooled by what it says on the back of the pack. If you're going to unmould your jellies (and you really should), you need to use more than it says. A good amount to use is 1 leaf for every 100ml/3½fl oz of liquid. This way, it will be easier to handle when you unmould it. A lesser amount – say, seven-tenths of a leaf per 100ml/3½fl oz – will create a jelly that will have little structural integrity for unmoulding but will be very tender: use this only for jellies set in glasses. Of course, the amount of gelatine required also depends on the proportions of the mould that you are using and the ingredients of the jelly: acid makes for a weaker gel; alcohol can strengthen a gel up to a point; and sugar makes a stronger gel too. (You'll find more information on gel strengths in the section on gelling agents, pp.144–146.) If in doubt, always err on the side of caution. It's better that your jelly is gracing your table, albeit a little firm, rather than relegated to the floor of your sink.

What sort of mould should I use?

When starting off, a tinned copper mould is ideal: if you haven't yet hit it big time and had a bespoke one made of your pet polar bear, don't worry. Old American aluminium moulds are good to use; in general, anything metal is a hot bet – although using a saucepan is perhaps a bit silly.

If you're out of metal moulds, go for plastic. You can use Tupperware or even the plastic moulds that supermarket foods come in. Now is not the time to dust down your granny's glass and ceramic mould collection. The impending disaster will put you off jellying for years. Later in the book, we'll explain how you can get your glass and ceramic moulds back into active service (p.147), but until then you'll have to be patient.

Can I make it set faster?

Yes. If you're short of time, stir the jelly mixture in a bowl set over another bowl half-filled with iced water. If you're really in a hurry, add a handful of salt to the iced water. Your jelly will start to set in minutes, but don't forget to stir: freezing destroys jelly. When the jelly starts to thicken and becomes slightly, but not too, lumpy, it can be poured into a mould. It will still take about 2 hours in the refrigerator to set firmly enough to be unmoulded. If you do need to make a jelly set in a hurry, you can always add some extra gelatine. This will help it gel quicker, but if you don't eat it quickly it will get significantly firmer the longer it stays in the refrigerator.

EASY FRUIT JELLIES

ORANGE JELLY

This tasty jelly blows children's party jelly out of the water. It's a great place to start exploring real jelly and it shows just how simple a fresh fruit jelly is to make.

FOR 500ML/18FL OZ. SERVES 4

JUICE FROM ABOUT 4 MEDIUM ORANGES (TO MAKE 300ML/10FL OZ)

JUICE OF ½ LEMON

100ML/3½ FL OZ SUGAR SYRUP (P.29)

100ML/3½ FL OZ WATER

5 LEAVES OF GELATINE

First the fun part: choose your mould! Use water and a measuring jug to check its volume. Then adjust the recipe as necessary. If you are going to fill glasses with the jelly, get these ready. Regardless of whether you are using a mould or glasses, it's a good idea to get into a habit of putting them on a tray to catch any accidental spills as you move the jelly to the refrigerator.

Cut the oranges in half and squeeze them, pips and all, into a measuring jug. Keep going until you have 300ml/10fl oz. Then squeeze in the lemon juice.

The orange juice is going to be relatively tart, so you will need to sweeten it. Add about equal quantities of syrup and water to the orange juice until you reach 500ml/18fl oz. If you think that you have exceptionally sweet oranges, then by all means add less syrup. In any case, the volume of the liquid must reach 500ml/18fl oz.

Now for turning it into a jelly. Cut the leaves of gelatine into a few pieces and place in a heatproof bowl. Add a few tablespoons of the juice mixture so that the gelatine is just covered. Let the gelatine soften for 10 minutes while you bring a small pan of water to a simmer.

Place the bowl of softened gelatine over the simmering water and stir from time to time until totally melted. This will take about 10 minutes. Pour the remainder of the juice mixture over the melted gelatine and stir to combine.

Finally, pour through a sieve into a measuring jug and then carefully fill your mould. Refrigerate until set.

EASY LEMON JELLY

Freshly made lemon jelly is utterly delicious. But if you use lemon juice, you will run into a couple of problems. The first is that lemon juice is a pale colour ; the second is that if you use too much lemon juice, there's a danger that its acidity will stop the gelatine doing its work. One way of getting a lovely yellow colour is by infusing lemon zest in sugar syrup; even simpler is to add a little bit of orange juice, which turns the jelly a radiant lemon yellow. This recipe is particularly good for children's palates – if you want something more grown up, then make the tart Lemonade Jelly (p.39).

FOR 500ML/18FL OZ. SERVES 4

125ML/4FL OZ LEMON JUICE

100ML/3½FL OZ ORANGE JUICE

125ML/4FL OZ SUGAR SYRUP (P.29)

150ML/5FL OZ WATER

5 LEAVES OF GELATINE

Squeeze the juices into a measuring jug and then add the sugar syrup and water.

Cut the leaves of gelatine into a few pieces and place in a heatproof bowl. Add a few tablespoons of the juice mixture so that the gelatine is just covered. Let the gelatine soften for 10 minutes whilst you bring a small pan of water to a simmer.

Place the bowl of softened gelatine over the simmering water and stir from time to time until totally melted. This takes about 10 minutes. Then pour the remainder of the juice mixture over the melted gelatine and stir to combine. Pour through a sieve into a jug and then carefully fill your mould. Refrigerate until set.

LEMONADE JELLY

Here's a fun recipe for making a really zingy lemon jelly. This is one that works best when it has an ultra-soft set, so it is best to set it in four wine glasses. The egg whites may seem strange, but they give it an incredible fizz.

First zest and juice the lemons, then put everything into a small saucepan along with the sugar and water. Heat up towards a simmer so that the sugar dissolves and the zest colours the liquid. Keep on a very low heat for an additional 5 minutes, then strain the liquid through a sieve to remove pips and zest. Add additional cold water to make 500ml/18fl oz.

Cut up 4 leaves of gelatine into a heatproof bowl and pour over a little of the lemon mixture. When the gelatine is soft, melt it over a pan of simmering water. Then pour over the rest of the lemon mixture and pour everything through a sieve into a clean bowl.

Put the egg whites into a bowl and then pour over the lemon mixture. Set this bowl over a larger bowl filled with ice water and whisk, using electric beaters, until the mixture has a got a good head of froth at the top and is just beginning to set. Don't go too far, or it will turn into a lemon mousse!

When the mixture feels cool to the touch, pour it into the four glasses. Obviously, this is a recipe where you don't need to skim the jelly before it sets.

FOR 500ML/18FL OZ. SERVES 4

JUICE AND ZEST OF 3 LEMONS

100G/3½OZ CASTER SUGAR

100ML/3½FL OZ WATER, PLUS EXTRA AS NECESSARY

4 LEAVES OF GELATINE

3 EGG WHITES

STRAWBERRY JELLY

Strawberry was one of the first jelly recipes we conquered. Back when we had real jobs we'd hit the wholesale market early to pick up crates of fruit. We would dress and juice the strawberries before heading into work – that way the fruit was in peak condition. We find that people get very into real strawberry jelly. They are so conditioned by artificial strawberry flavours that the real flavour is a wake up call.

So far, we have dealt with making jellies using easily obtainable juice. Some fruits are harder to juice than an orange, so you'll need a different method. The best way of getting juice out of soft fruits like strawberries and raspberries is to heat them gently in a bowl set over simmering water until the juices flood out.

Start by juicing the strawberries. It is easiest to do this a day ahead if possible. Hull and chop the strawberries and place in a heatproof bowl. Then add the sugar and the lemon juice. The lemon juice is important, as it cuts through the richness of the strawberry juice and balances the flavour. Cover the top of the bowl with clingfilm – make sure that both the bowl and clingfilm are heat-resistant. Place the bowl above a pan of simmering water, and give it a good shake from time to time so that the strawberries are heated evenly. It will take about 30 minutes for the juice to be released.

You'll be left with a bowl of vibrantly coloured juice and a whole heap of strawberry pulp. To separate the juice from the strawberries, it is best to use a jelly bag. A jelly bag is a very fine fabric sieve, which over the course of many hours will let the juice drip out beautifully clear.

FOR 500ML/18FL OZ. SERVES 4

450G/1LB RIPE STRAWBERRIES

55G/2OZ CASTER SUGAR

JUICE OF ½ LEMON

ABOUT 300ML/10FL OZ WATER

5 LEAVES OF GELATINE

RECIPE CONTINUES OVERLEAF >

If you don't have a jelly bag, line a sieve with an old — but clean — tea towel and set over a bowl. The juice will be at it clearest only if you let gravity do the work. If you're in a rush, you could use a few strokes of a wooden spoon to encourage the juice through — but don't go over the top.

Depending on the fruitiness of the strawberries, you should be left with about 200ml/7fl oz of juice. Add water to bring the volume up to 500ml/18fl oz of liquid. (If you have less than that amount of juice, simply add more water.)

To set the jelly, cut up the gelatine and cover with about 2 tablespoons of the strawberry juice mixture and allow to soften. Then place over a pan of simmering water until it has dissolved. Finally add the rest of the strawberry juice mixture, stir and then pass through a sieve into a suitable mould. Refrigerate until set.

A great use of the leftover strawberries (or indeed any other soft fruit) is to make them into a sorbet. It's really easy. Place the pulp in a food processor and combine with icing sugar and the juice of a whole lemon until the mixture is smooth and sweet. Then tip into a shallow plastic container. Place this in the freezer and whisk vigorously with a fork every few hours until it is totally frozen. Easier still is to freeze in an ice-cream machine.

RHUBARB AND ROSÉ JELLY

For this jelly recipe, you release the juice from the rhubarb by stewing it. Stewing also works well to release juice from fruits such as plums, cherries and blueberries. Many will be familiar with stewing rhubarb, but putting the juice to use in a jelly makes for a sublime experience. Even if it is pink and throbbing.

FOR 500ML/18FL OZ. SERVES 4

1KG/2LB 4OZ RHUBARB

200ML/7FL OZ WATER

175G/6 OZ CASTER SUGAR

1 STAR ANISE

JUICE OF ½ LEMON

125ML/4FL OZ ROSÉ WINE OR WATER

5 LEAVES OF GELATINE

Wash and trim the rhubarb. Cut into 5cm/2in lengths, and add to a saucepan. Add the water, sugar and star anise. Bring to the boil and cover. Simmer until the rhubarb is really soft. This takes about 30 minutes.

Line a sieve with a clean tea towel and set over a bowl. Decant the rhubarb to the sieve and let the juice work its way through. You'll be left with a beautiful neon pink juice. To this add the lemon juice.

Measure the volume of the rhubarb juice. If you are going down the rosé route, use 375ml/13fl oz of juice with 125ml/4fl oz of rosé. Cheers! And if you are going the teetotal route, use as much rhubarb juice as you have and top up with water as necessary to bring it to 500ml/18fl oz.

Cut the leaves of gelatine into a few pieces and place in a heatproof bowl. Add a few tablespoons of the juice mixture so that the gelatine is just covered. Let the gelatine soften for 10 minutes whilst you bring a small pan of water to a simmer. Then place the bowl of softened gelatine over the simmering water and stir from time to time until totally melted.

Pour the remainder of the juice mixture over the melted gelatine and stir to combine. Finally, pour the mixture through a sieve into a jug and then carefully fill your mould. Refrigerate until set.

CHERRY JELLY

Cherry jelly is really good. Sam thinks it's the best fruit jelly ever. This recipe uses a very fine cherry purée to create an unusual fruity texture. It's simple to make, as you can add the cherries directly to a saucepan without worrying about the stones.

Place the washed cherries into a saucepan and add the water and sugar. Bring to a boil, then cover and simmer gently until very soft – about 45 minutes.

Pass the juice through a sieve, pushing down with the back of a wooden spoon, until you have a bowl of rich cherry pulp. To this, add the lemon juice. Old recipes suggest that this is the time to add a brandy glass of Kirsch. This is suitably ambiguous, so interpret as you see fit. In any case, add additional water until you reach 500ml/18fl oz.

Cut the leaves of gelatine into a few pieces and place in a heatproof bowl. Add a few tablespoons of the juice mixture so that the gelatine is just covered. Let the gelatine soften for 10 minutes while you bring a small pan of water to a simmer. Then place the bowl of softened gelatine over the simmering water and stir from time to time until totally melted. Pour the remainder of the juice mixture over the melted gelatine and stir.

Finally, pour the mixture through a sieve into a jug and then carefully fill your mould. Refrigerate until set.

FOR 500ML/18FL OZ. SERVES 4

400G/14OZ CHERRIES

150ML/5FL OZ WATER

75G/2¾ OZ CASTER SUGAR

JUICE OF ½ LEMON

ADDITIONAL WATER AND OPTIONAL KIRSCH

5 LEAVES OF GELATINE

Greengage Jelly

It's a shame that greengages are in season for such a small part of the year as they are really tasty. In late summer, greengages make an unusual jelly. It's worth making extra juice and freezing it for later in the year.

Slice the greengages into quarters, removing the stones as you go, and place in a saucepan. Cover with the water and sugar, then bring to the boil and simmer covered until they have broken down – about 10 minutes.

Pour the contents into a colander lined with a clean tea towel. Use a wooden spoon to encourage the juices to go through, although this should happen without much difficulty. Then measure out 325ml/11½ fl oz and add the Riesling or water to make up to 500ml/18fl oz.

Cut the leaves of gelatine into a few pieces and place in a heatproof bowl. Add a few tablespoons of the juice mixture so that the gelatine is just covered. Let the gelatine soften for 10 minutes while you bring a small pan of water to a simmer. Then place the bowl of softened gelatine over the simmering water and stir from time to time until totally melted. Pour the remainder of the juice mixture over the melted gelatine and stir to combine.

Finally, pour through a sieve into a jug and then carefully fill your mould. Place in the refrigerator to set.

FOR 500ML/18FL OZ. SERVES 4

500G/1LB 2OZ RIPE GREENGAGES
(OR OTHER PLUMS)

200ML/7FL OZ WATER

50G/1¾ OZ CASTER SUGAR

175ML/6FL OZ RIESLING OR WATER

5 LEAVES OF GELATINE

PINEAPPLE JELLY

Those used to children's jelly cubes may be familiar with the warning not to set fresh pineapple, papaya or kiwi fruit in the jelly. These exotic fruits contain enzymes that attack gelatine and prevent it from forming a proper gel. Bromelian, the enzyme in pineapple responsible for this, is literally flesh-eating! Fran Beauman, who has written on the subject, reports that a particularly vicious pineapple can make your mouth bleed!

Flesh-eating aside, the history of the pineapple is quite intriguing. At one time, pineapples were so rare and in vogue that in 1761 a giant stone folly was built in the shape of one at Dunmore Park, Scotland. Back in the kitchen, it occurs again and again as a motif for jelly moulds.

To make a pineapple jelly set, you need to first denature the enzyme. Sounds complicated, but it only involves heating up the juice. This is why you can use canned pineapple in jelly: the fruit is pasteurized during canning.

FOR 500ML/18FL OZ. SERVES 4

1 LARGE RIPE PINEAPPLE

200ML/7FL OZ WATER

75G/2¾ OZ CASTER SUGAR

JUICE OF 1 LIME

ADDITIONAL WATER (SEE RECIPE)

5 LEAVES OF GELATINE

Peel the pineapple and do your best to remove the eyes. Remove the core and discard. Cut the flesh into chunks and add to a saucepan. Then cover with the water and sugar and bring to the boil. Simmer gently, covered, until the pineapple is cooked right through – about 45 minutes.

Tip the stewed pineapple and juice into a sieve set over a bowl. Add the lime juice and make up to 500ml/18fl oz by adding more water.

Cut the leaves of gelatine into a few pieces and place in a heatproof bowl. Add a few tablespoons of the juice mixture so that the gelatine is just covered. Let the gelatine soften for 10 minutes whilst you bring a small pan of water to a simmer. Place the bowl of softened gelatine over the simmering water and stir from time to time until totally melted. Then pour the remainder of the juice mixture over the melted gelatine and stir to combine.

Pour through a sieve into a jug and then carefully fill your mould. Refrigerate until set. If you wish you can set the stewed pineapple into the jelly (see method on p.64).

Um Bongo Jelly

This is the Tarzan of jellies. As childhood fans of the exotic and improbably named Um Bongo tropical drink ('Um Bongo, Um Bongo, they drink it in the Congo'), we had to have a tropical jelly recipe to take you back to the '80s. For our tropical jelly, we've gone with pineapple, passion fruit, lemon, lime and oranges – but there are infinitely more combinations up for grabs.

FOR 500ML/18FL OZ, SERVES 4

1 SMALL RIPE PINEAPPLE

JUICE OF 1 LARGE ORANGE

JUICE OF 1 LEMON

JUICE AND ZEST OF 1 LIME

3 PASSION FRUITS

5 LEAVES OF GELATINE

ADDITIONAL WATER (SEE RECIPE)

75G/2¾ OZ CASTER SUGAR

Start by dealing with the pineapple as in the recipe for Pineapple Jelly (see p.50).

Once you have the clear pineapple juice, add the orange, lemon and lime juice, the lime zest and then the juice of the passion fruits. Hold back the passion fruit seeds and set aside for later. Make up to 500ml/18fl oz using water as necessary.

Cut the leaves of gelatine into a few pieces and place in a heatproof bowl. Add a few tablespoons of the juice mixture so that the gelatine is just covered. Let the gelatine soften for 10 minutes while you bring a small pan of water to a simmer. Place the bowl of softened gelatine over the simmering water and stir from time to time until totally melted. Then pour the remainder of the juice mixture over the melted gelatine and stir to combine. Pour through a sieve into a bowl.

Set the bowl over a larger bowl filled with ice water. This will speed up the gelling process and allow the passion fruit seeds to be incorporated. After about 15 minutes, the mixture should be sufficiently gelled so that you can stir in the seeds without them sinking to the bottom. At this point, tip the jelly into a mould and place in the refrigerator to fully set.

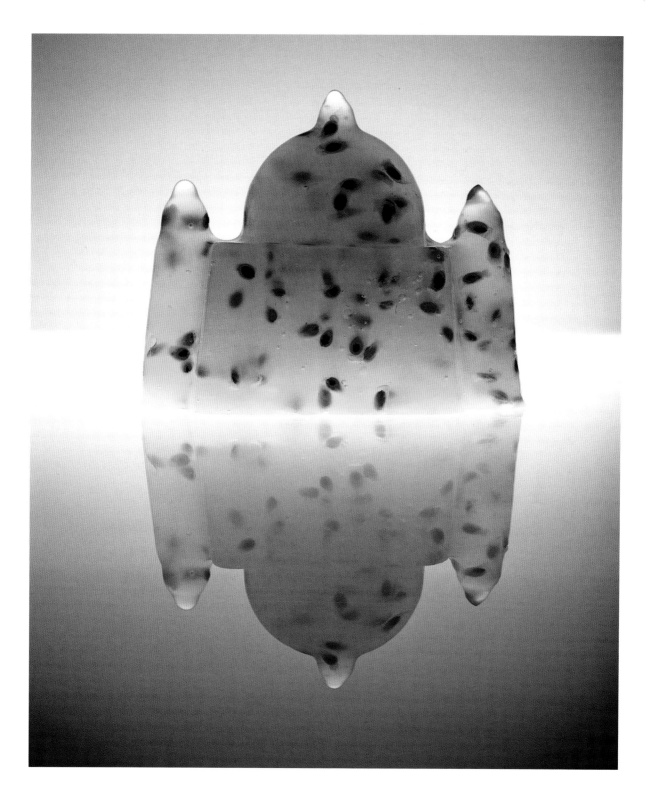

Technique Jellies

RIBBAND JELLY

Ribband Jelly is the traditional name for a striped jelly. In the past, making complex jellies often involved just one batch of jelly, which was then divided so that flavours and colours could be added to create different jellies.

You can set any colour of jelly in layers, although you will get the best results when you use a clear jelly in combination with an opaque jelly. That way, the colours don't merge into one. A raspberry and blancmange duo is a good place to start. Start by making the raspberry jelly and, while you are waiting for the juice to strain, get started on the blancmange jelly (recipes overleaf).

Choose a suitable mould and place it in the freezer to get it really cold. Something with a hole in the middle that can be filled with fruit and cream is a fun way to go. *This recipe will give you a 1 litre/1¼ pint Ribband Jelly, which serves 8.*

TO ASSEMBLE THE RIBBAND JELLY

You should have two jugs of unset jelly and a thoroughly freezing mould.

Start by pouring a layer of the blancmange into the mould. Place in the refrigerator until set. This should take only 15 minutes.

Continue adding and setting contrasting layers to the jelly until it is full. You can make the layers as thin or thick as you like. Thin layers set quicker but you will need to pour more of them; thicker layers set more slowly but there are less of them to do.

When all the layers are complete, continue to let the jelly chill for about another 2 hours to firm it up before unmoulding and serving. A mound of whipped cream topped with a pile of raspberries will show off your spectacular creation best.

CONTINUES OVERLEAF >

Raspberry jelly

Rinse the raspberries and place them, along with the sugar, in a heatproof bowl. Cover tightly with clingfilm and place on top of a pan of simmering water. Let the heat release the juices from the berries; this will take about 30 minutes. When you've got a nice pool of juice, pour the lot into a sieve lined with a clean tea towel and let the juice drip through clear.

Once the juice is strained, add the lemon juice and the water to bring the volume up to 500ml/18fl oz.

Cut the leaves of gelatine into a few pieces and place in a heatproof bowl. Add a few tablespoons of the juice mixture so that the gelatine is just covered. Let the gelatine soften for 10 minutes whilst you bring a small pan of water to a simmer. Place the bowl of gelatine over the simmering water and stir from time to time until totally melted. Pour the remainder of the juice mixture over the gelatine, stir to combine and sieve into a jug.

FOR 500ML/18FL OZ JELLY

450G/1LB RIPE ENGLISH RASPBERRIES

75G/2¾ OZ CASTER SUGAR

JUICE OF ½ LEMON

ABOUT 300ML/10FL OZ WATER

5 LEAVES OF GELATINE

Blancmange jelly

Gelatine-based blancmanges made with whole milk will set a little firmer than fruit jellies, so it's OK to use a little less gelatine. This keeps the mouthfeel suitably soft.

Start by chopping the gelatine into a heatproof bowl and add the water, along with the sugar and the lemon zest. Wait 10 minutes for the gelatine to soften and then heat over a pan of simmering water until the gelatine has melted. It is possible to melt the gelatine in the milk but it takes a long time – so it's easier to use water.

Once the gelatine has melted, add the milk to the bowl, stir to combine, and pass the lot through a sieve and into a jug.

FOR 500ML/18FL OZ BLANCMANGE

4 LEAVES OF GELATINE

100ML/3½ FL OZ WATER

1 TBSP CASTER SUGAR

ZEST OF ½ LEMON

400ML/13½ FL OZ WHOLE MILK

MARBLING

Harry's always had an unhealthy fascination with the theory of taste embodied in marbled foods. Just think of Kobe beef or Stilton cheese: they look marbled and are full of flavour. The Victorians evidently thought so too as they made marbled jellies. We found an old recipe for Marble Sweet Jelly whilst looking through *The Encyclopedia of Practical Cookery*, published in 1892. For a taste of how jelly recipes used to be written, here's the recipe quoted in full:

> **MARBLED SWEET JELLY.** *Get a jelly mould, put some pieces of different kinds of jelly at the bottom, over these pour some jelly that has had milk or cream mixed with it to make it white, so as to form the veins of the marble; the jelly should only just be liquid, for if it is too warm it will melt the other jelly, and spoil the effect. Let the jelly get cool as quickly as possible, then proceed as before, continuing in that way till the mould is full; pack the mould in ice and leave till the jelly is quite set. When ready, dip the mould in tepid water, wipe it, and turn the jelly out onto a glass dish.*

To make the marbled jelly, you need to make three different jellies. Two should be brightly coloured and fully set before you start work on the blancmange part. It's a good way of using up any leftover jelly.

CONTINUES OVERLEAF >

MARBLED JELLY

Blueberry jelly (opposite) and lemon jelly (see p.36) make a good combination to serve with delicious cardamom and honey blancmange (opposite). Make the jellies first and ensure they are fully set before starting the blancmange. Use a half quantity of the recipe for lemon jelly on p.36 to give you about 250ml/9fl oz. *This recipe will give you a 1 litre/1¼ pint Marbled Jelly, which serves 8.*

TO ASSEMBLE THE MARBLED JELLY

Gather your lemon and blueberry jellies. Turn them out onto a chopping board and cut them into small squares, triangles and strips. You need 250ml/9fl oz of each chopped jelly.

Stir the blancmange mix occasionally until it starts to get lumpy. This shouldn't take more than 15 minutes. At this point, you can add the chopped jelly and the almonds. As the mixture is quite thick, they will end up distributed evenly.

Pour the setting mixture into an elegant mould and place in the refrigerator. It will be ready for unmoulding in about 4 hours.

BLUEBERRY JELLY

Place the washed blueberries, water and sugar in a saucepan. Pop on a lid and stew for 10 minutes, or until the blueberries have split and lost their shape. Strain everything through a sieve and into a measuring jug until you have 250ml/9fl oz of liquid – add water if necessary.

Cut up the gelatine into a heatproof bowl, add a little of the blueberry mixture, and leave to soften. Place the softened bowl of gelatine over a pan of boiling water and allow to melt. Once melted, pour over the rest of the blueberry mixture and pour through a sieve back into the measuring jug.

If you want it to set quickly, pour thin layers onto a couple of dinner plates and refrigerate until firm.

FOR 250ML/9FL OZ JELLY

125G/4½ OZ BLUEBERRIES

100ML/3½ FL OZ WATER

2 TBSP CASTER SUGAR

2½ LEAVES OF GELATINE

CARDAMOM & HONEY BLANCMANGE

First you need to infuse the milk. Put the milk in a saucepan with the cardamom, lemon zest and honey and heat until it is just about to simmer. Remove from the heat and allow the flavour to infuse as the mixture cools – about 20 minutes.

Meanwhile, cut the gelatine into a heatproof bowl and cover with the water. When the gelatine has softened, heat the mixture over simmering water until the gelatine is melted. Pour the infused milk over the melted gelatine and stir to combine, then pour through a sieve and into a bowl.

Place the bowl over a larger bowl filled with ice.

FOR 500ML/18FL OZ BLANCMANGE

400ML/13½ FL OZ WHOLE MILK

10 CARDAMOM PODS

ZEST OF 1 LEMON

50G/1¾ OZ HONEY

4½ LEAVES OF GELATINE

100ML/3½ FL OZ WATER

1 TBSP SLICED BLANCHED ALMONDS

SETTING FRUIT IN JELLY

Sometimes jellies are at their most stunning when they have fruit set inside them. We've found that one of the most popular recipes is elderflower jelly with raspberries set in it. If you can get hold of a combination of yellow and red raspberries, so much the better.

To make the elderflower jelly, you need to make up some elderflower cordial. Before you do this, don't forget that flavours diminish with cold, so you need to make the cordial stronger than you would normally. Otherwise, the taste might be too subtle. The joy of using cordial is that it is already a sugar syrup, so you won't need to add anything to make it sweeter.

ELDERFLOWER & RASPBERRY

FOR 500ML/18FL OZ

150ML/5FL OZ ELDERFLOWER
CORDIAL

350ML/12FL OZ WATER

5 LEAVES OF GELATINE

125G/4½ OZ (1 PUNNET)
RASPBERRIES OR OTHER SOFT FRUIT

First, in a jug, mix the cordial with the water. Cut up the gelatine and add to a heatproof bowl. Just cover with a splash of the cordial mixture and leave for 10 minutes to soften. Then place the bowl over a pan of simmering water and allow the gelatine to melt. Next, pour over the remainder of the cordial, stir, and pass through a sieve back into the jug.

Carefully rinse the raspberries to remove any dirt and discard any overly soft berries, then place them into the mould.

When you have made up the jelly, you can begin filling the mould. Fill the mould only half full. Raspberries are fairly buoyant, so if you half-fill the mould and then allow this to set, you will end up with a jelly with fruit held aloft.

Meanwhile, keep the remaining mixture at room temperature. After a few hours in the refrigerator, the jelly will have set sufficiently for you to pour the remaining mixture into the mould. On a really cold day, the mixture in the jug might start to gel. If this happens, melt it by putting the jug in a pan of hot water for a few minutes. Once the final layer has set, you are ready to unmould.

MOSAIC JELLY

Mosaic jellies are one of the most spectacular things that you can do without a complex mould. The idea is that you line the interior of the mould with thin tiles of jelly. Of course, the mosaic can be as complicated as you like. A good way to start is to use cookie cutters to create the jelly tiles. We've used a fleur-de-lis cutter, which we designed. Harry got it made on a machine that is normally used for making replacement body parts, you know, titanium hip joints and the like. You can use anything you like: just alter the colours and shapes to suit the occasion. Or cut out shapes with a knife or other tool.

Sticking cut out shapes onto the interior of a mould is quite an art, so to get started it's easier to make the jelly on a flat tray. The results will still be spectacular. Once you are practised – try moulds with curved or domed sides.

FOR THE JELLY TILES

Start by making a blancmange jelly (p.59) and setting the jelly into thin (about 4mm/slightly thinner than ¼ in) sheets on a flat, and super clean, baking tray. It may be easier to use a series of flat dinner plates. Make the jelly using 5 leaves of gelatine per 500ml/18fl oz of liquid so that it is a bit firmer. This will make it easier to cut and lift the shapes.

Choose a flat dish in which to set the jelly. Metal trays really do work best here because it is easier to stick the jelly shapes onto them.

ASSEMBLING THE MOSAIC

Carefully cut out shapes from the blancmange and transfer them to the dish using a palette knife. Then arrange the shapes as you see fit. Place back in the refrigerator for 30 minutes to firm up a little.

Carefully fill the dish with a jelly of your choice. If you are using white tiles, a strawberry jelly would make a good contrast. The trick is to get the filling jelly a little viscous before adding it: this stops the mosaic from floating away.

Once set, serve at the table to amaze your dinner guests.

STRIPED CLEMENTINE JELLIES

Many people will remember eating sail boats made from jellies set inside oranges, with sails made from rice paper and cocktail sticks. In fact, setting jellies into hollowed-out oranges has quite a heritage. The great chef Antonin Carême made the ultimate combination, magically setting thin layers of jelly inside hollowed-out clementines. We picked up this technique from the wonderful food historian Ivan Day. Try it: it's not as complicated as it looks and the results are spectacular. Make sure that you reveal the layered jelly with a ceremonial slicing at the table.

When you are out shopping, choose clementines that have lots of give in the peel. Otherwise, this recipe is just no fun.

1. HOLLOWING OUT THE CLEMENTINES

First find the right end of the clementine: you want the bit that sticks out a little and has the dark hard bit where it was attached to the tree. Use a small knife to remove a circle of peel about 15mm/slightly larger than ½in in diameter. From this, you are going to hollow out the clementine.

Using a small teaspoon, carefully remove the segments from the clementines. Once you've got the first segment out, it gets easier. Keep removing the flesh until the clementine is cleanly hollowed out. Don't worry if you create small holes: these can be fixed. But don't rip the sides, so careful as you go! Place the flesh into a bowl. This will be made into the clementine jelly. Meanwhile, refrigerate the clementine skins. This will make setting the layers quicker.

2. MAKING THE CLEMENTINE JELLY

Pass the clementine flesh through the sieve and into a measuring jug until you have obtained all the juices. Now add half sugar syrup and half water until you have doubled the liquid in volume. Use the Universal

FOR 10 CLEMENTINES:

FOR THE CLEMENTINE JELLY:	FOR THE BLANCMANGE:
10 CLEMENTINES	8 LEAVES OF GELATINE
SUGAR SYRUP (P.29) (FOR QUANTITY SEE METHOD)	200ML/7FL OZ WATER
WATER (FOR QUANTITY SEE METHOD)	1 TBSP CASTER SUGAR
GELATINE LEAVES, QUANTITY TO SUIT (SEE UNIVERSAL	ZEST OF ½ LEMON
RECIPE, PP.24—28)	800ML/1½ PINTS MILK

CONTINUES OVERLEAF >

Jelly recipe (see pp.24–28) to add the correct quantity of gelatine and get the jelly mixture made up. Keep this in a jug.

3. MAKING THE BLANCMANGE

Make up an equal quantity of blancmange, following the recipe on p.59.

4. FIXING ANY HOLES IN THE CLEMENTINES

The next stage is to fix any tiny holes in the bottom of the clementines. We're going to block them with jelly. To do this, take a few tablespoons of the clementine jelly, then put it into a glass and place in the refrigerator. Don't forget about it. In about 15 minutes, it will have gelled enough so that it can be used to block the holes. You want it lumpy but still just about flowing.

Place a small amount of the clementine jelly into any holes that need blocking and place back in the refrigerator until fully set. This will take about 15 minutes.

5. SETTING THE LAYERS

Once you are watertight, you can get going on the layers. For the first layer, measure 1 tablespoon of clementine jelly and pour it into the clementines. Allow to set. As the layers are thin, this should take no more than 30 minutes. Then follow with 1 tablespoon of the blancmange and again allow to set.

If any of the jelly in the jugs begins to gel during this process, heat it up gently by immersing in a pan of lukewarm water.

Keep adding alternate layers of jelly until the clementines are full. Try to end with a clementine layer.

6. THE REVEAL

To serve, simply slice the clementines top to bottom into quarters to reveal the magical stripes. Eat like half-time oranges.

It is, of course, possible to do this with other flavours, but it does make sense to use the juice that you get from the clementines. Mixing the orange juice with some strawberry juice works well, as it increases the colour contrast with the blancmange.

GOLD LEAF IN JELLIES

Cooking with gold leaf is a total extravagance: it doesn't improve the jelly since it has no smell or perceptible taste, and it is a complete bore to handle. It does, however, massively increase the impact of the jelly: the extravagance of eating 24-carat gold adds a frisson, and it looks splendid if done properly.

If you have any qualms about eating gold, don't worry. It's totally inert and the European Union recognizes it as a food additive (E175), though this rather knocks the glamour out of it. More excitingly, as it's inert your body can't digest any – and you can imagine what that means.

Gold leaf has a glorious history in cooking. In the Middle Ages, whole birds, pâtés and pigs' heads were wrapped in gold leaf for feasting. In 1769, Elizabeth Raffald wrote a recipe for gilded fish in jelly. Once you've unmoulded your fish you carefully lay gold leaf onto them, arrange them in a dish and flood the plate with jelly. These days, gold is used sparingly to decorate chocolates and in the liqueur Danziger Goldwasser. But once you finish reading this segment, you will be able to achieve far more spectacular effects with gold.

You can get hold of gold from large art shops and even builder's merchants. It comes in three different formats: gold leaf, gold ribbon and gold dust. We use gold leaf because it is the best value for money at under £1 per leaf. You get 25 leaves per booklet and it represents the best return on investment in terms of absolute impact.

The higher carat of gold, the better. Anything above 22-carat gold is edible, but the closer it is to 24-carat, the better. Below 24 carats, the gold is mixed with copper and nickel. We tend to use 22.5-carat gold.

See overleaf for the technique.

SETTING GOLD LEAF
IN A GEL

Rather than make a jelly recipe that has gold throughout, it is often most effective to concentrate the gold at the top of the jelly for maximum impact. If you are going to unmould your jelly, put the gold gel in first; if the jelly is being served inside a glass, put it in last.

ENOUGH TO TIP 10 SMALL JELLIES

2 LEAVES OF GELATINE

100ML/3½FL OZ PROSECCO OR
SUGAR SYRUP (P.29)

10 SHEETS OF GOLD LEAF

Sam likes to set gold gel firmer than the rest of the jelly; Harry thinks this is a habit gained from the first gold jellies that Sam made – they were jelly breasts with golden nipples … For best results, you want the gold leaf suspended throughout the gel, and for this to happen the gel has to thicken slightly. This is super-quick if you have a higher gel to fluid ratio.

Cut the gelatine into a bowl, add a splash of prosecco and let the leaves soften. Melt the gelatine over a pan of simmering water, add the rest of the prosecco and strain back into a jug.

Now you have the gel to which you can add the gold. Gold leaf is only a few atoms thick, so it's very fragile. You need to manipulate 10 leaves of it from its booklet and into the mixture. You could use a gilders tip (made out of squirrel hair), but we tend to use a fork with a slightly damp tine. It's easier.

Hold the booklet of gold leaf right over the jug. Use the moistened fork to pick up corners of gold leaf and pull them into the liquid. Gold leaf will stick to anything that it lands on, so try to get it into the liquid first time.

When the 10 sheets of gold leaf are in the jug, use a whisk to beat it up. The aim is to break up the gold leaf into tiny fragments that will catch the light, but to avoid introducing air bubbles into the mix. Tilt the jug to pick up any gold leaf that has stuck to the sides and beat it in.

When the gold leaf has been broken up to a size you are happy with, lower the temperature of the mixture by holding it over an ice bath or in your refrigerator until it has gelled sufficiently that when the gold is stirred round it no longer sinks to the bottom of the mixture. When it is at this consistency, pour it swiftly into the mould and refrigerate until this layer is set.

If the gelling goes too far and the mixture sets (or is too thick to pour), you can rescue it! Jelly is very forgiving. Hold the mixing jug in a bowl of hot water and stir until it reaches the desired consistency. *See the Funeral Jelly recipe on p.112 for a full recipe with gold.*

ALCOHOLIC JELLIES

WEDDING JELLY

Wedding cakes are all stodge and no fun. It's inexplicable that people spend so much on vast monstrosities of fruit cake shrouded in royal icing. After all, most of it never gets eaten: it's trodden into the dance floor, stuffed in handbags and left forgotton in an attic in anticipation of a christening. Wedding jellies, on the other hand, are lighter and more refreshing than fruit cakes. And they are kinder to the stomach after a heavy meal, making it less likely that guests will fall asleep duing the speeches!

After making a towering jelly for the wedding of Sam's cousin, we decided to launch a wedding jelly service. There's been a freeing up of what's acceptable to serve at weddings, and we've been to events where cheese, cupcakes and even meat pies are served in lieu of a wedding cake.

Try the following recipe for a Champagne and summer fruit wedding jelly and your guests won't be disappointed.

CHAMPAGNE & SUMMER FRUIT WEDDING JELLY

A bottle of Champagne will make enough jelly for four proper servings and a glass for yourself while you are cooking. Make sure to chill the Champagne ahead of time – it's important that you drink whilst on the job.

FOR 500ML/18FL OZ. ENOUGH FOR 4

5 LEAVES OF GELATINE

450ML/16FL OZ CHAMPAGNE OR SPARKLING WINE

40G/1½OZ CASTER SUGAR

A SQUEEZE OF LEMON JUICE

A HANDFUL OF SMALL FRUIT (BLUEBERRIES, RASPBERRIES, GRAPES …WHATEVER LOOKS GOOD)

Cut the leaf gelatine into a heatproof bowl with a pair of scissors. Add enough Champagne to cover (about 100ml/3½fl oz). Leave the gelatine to soften for 10 minutes.

Bring a pan of water to the boil and place the bowl of softened gelatine on top of the pan of boiling water. Once the gelatine has totally melted, stir in the sugar until it has dissolved and add another 100ml/3½fl oz of Champagne to the mixture.

Combine the mixture with the rest of the Champagne by pouring it through a sieve – to remove any unmelted lumps – and into a measuring jug. Squeeze the lemon through the sieve too. Top up with Champagne until you have 500ml/18fl oz.

Place the washed fruit into the bottom of the mould and pour in about one-third of the jelly. Put the mould in the refrigerator for the jelly to set. Leave until set enough so that the fruit seems safely embedded (about 2 hours), then pour over the rest of the jelly mixture and return to the refrigerator.

If you don't want to set the fruit in the mould first, you can always add everything to the mould at once. Doing a double set, however, makes sure that the fruit floats elegantly in the unmoulded jelly rather than sinking to the bottom. For a way of keeping all the fizz in the Champagne, see p.132.

ABSINTHE JELLY RONSON

We created Jelly Ronson for Mark Ronson's 33rd birthday party. Historically, chefs have named foods to honor patrons. Antonin Carême created a Soufflé Rothschild in the 1820s and Auguste Escoffier, chef of the Savoy Hotel, created Peach Melba in the early 1890s to honour the Australian soprano Dame Nellie Melba. It's still popular.

This alcoholic jelly is fully potent. Sam likes to serve it to make sure that parties kick off; things can get a little wild after it's introduced. And if you are making it for a party, it's worthwhile covering any paintings and wall decorations you value. If this jelly is served after 11pm, food *will* be thrown. Remember, 11pm is the witching hour for throwing food.

Prepare this at least a day before serving. Which leaves you free on the day to organize your party.

For the Jelly

150ML/5FL OZ ABSINTHE
(BOHEMIAN ABSINTHE PREFERRED)

300ML/10FL OZ INDIAN TONIC WATER

JUICE OF ½ LIME

50ML/2FL OZ SUGAR SYRUP (P.29)

5 LEAVES OF GELATINE

Combine the absinthe, Indian tonic water, lime juice and sugar syrup in a jug and set aside. Cut the leaf gelatine into pieces and place in a heat-proof bowl with enough of the cocktail mixture to submerse. Leave until soft.

When the gelatine has softened, melt it by placing the bowl over a pan of simmering water. Then add the remainder of the absinthe cocktail, give it a brief stir and pour the lot through a sieve and back into the jug. Find a suitably extravagent mould and fill it with the mixture. Refrigerate overnight to set – now you've got a whole day to cover up those paintings.

For the Raspberry Coulis

60G/2¼ OZ RASPBERRIES

JUICE OF ½ LEMON

1 TSP ICING SUGAR

We serve this with a raspberry coulis.

Place the raspberries, lemon juice and icing sugar into the small bowl of a food processor and whizz until smooth. Use a spoon to force the coulis through a sieve, into a bowl and thence into a small jug. Job done!

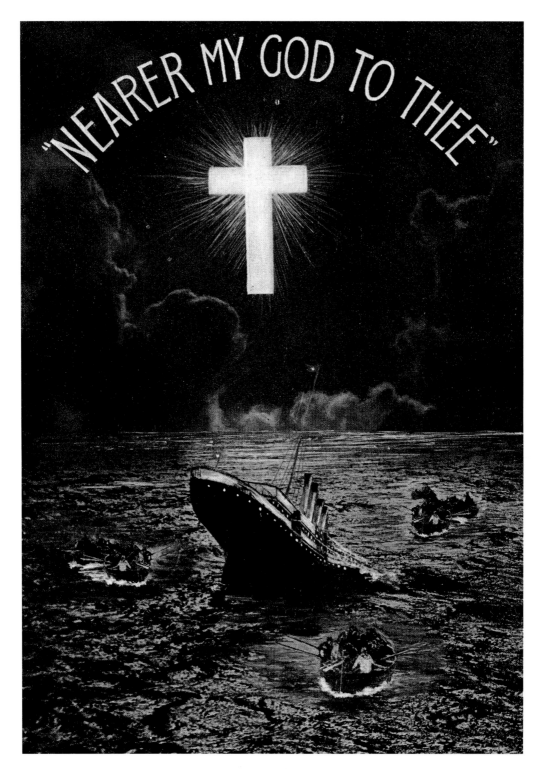

TITANIC JELLY

For 2000 years, last suppers have been some of the most interesting meals around. Everyone has a last supper waiting for them, though most don't feature jelly. Some death row inmates have had a crack but their jellies have been pretty un-ambitious; the same is not true of the jellies that were eaten by passengers the night the Titanic sank. The story of the Titanic is endlessly fascinating; after all, this is still the ultimate shipwreck. Only two menus survive from the night of 14 April, 1912. The menu from First Class features a jelly for the tenth course. One of the passengers, Mrs Jacques Futrelle, described the scene:

> *There was not the slightest thought of danger in the minds of those who sat around the tables in the luxurious dining saloon of the Titanic. It was a brilliant crowd. Jewels flashed from the gowns of the women. And, oh, the dear women, how fondly they wore their latest Parisian gowns! It was the first time that most of them had an opportunity to display their newly acquired finery.*

The guests that tucked into the jelly that night included some of the ship's most renowned passengers: John Jacob Astor, Benjamin Guggenheim, and Isidor and Ida Straus. It was a splendid feast, and by the time they got to the jelly they would have been stuffed. No doubt they would have been grateful to be presented with a light peach and chartreuse jelly before getting stuck into coffee and cigars. If you are having a last supper, you could do a lot worse.

Several hours later, in the early morning of 15 April, the *Titanic* sank, taking 1581 passengers and crew with her. The band played the hymn "Nearer, My God, To Thee" as the ship went down.

CONTINUES OVERLEAF >

CHARTREUSE & PEACH JELLY

This recipe is taken from the surreal book *Last Dinner on the Titanic*. Every year groups of enthusiasts recreate the menus from the doomed liner and even get involved in aristocratic role-play. This jelly is good with cigars and impending doom at the end of the meal.

FOR THE POACHED PEACHES

For Poached Peaches

2 LARGE PEACHES

500ML/18FL OZ WATER

250G/9OZ CASTER SUGAR

2 WHOLE CLOVES

1 CINNAMON STICK

JUICE OF ½ LEMON

First, peel the peaches by immersing them in boiling water for 30 seconds. Take them out and plunge them into cold water before removing the skins, halving the fruit and taking out the stones.

Combine the water and sugar in a pan and heat until the sugar has dissolved. Add the cloves, cinnamon and lemon juice. Bring the syrup just to the boil and then reduce the heat. Add the peaches and poach for 6 minutes, or until they are soft. Remove the peaches, but don't throw away the syrup.

FOR THE JELLY

For the Jelly

FOR 500ML/18FL OZ, ENOUGH FOR 4

200ML/7FL OZ CHARTREUSE LIQUEUR

250ML/9FL OZ WATER

50ML/2FL OZ PEACH POACHING SYRUP OR SUGAR SYRUP (P.29)

5 LEAVES OF GELATINE

PEACHES, PREPARED AS ABOVE, OR 100G/3½OZ CANNED PEACHES

In a jug, combine the Chartreuse liqueur, water and 50ml/2fl oz of the poaching syrup.

Cut the leaf gelatine into a heatproof bowl and add enough water to cover. Leave the gelatine to soften for 10 minutes.

Bring a pan of water to the boil and place the bowl of softened gelatine on top of the pan. Once the gelatine has totally melted, add the rest of the Chartreuse mixture and give it a quick stir.

Pour a shallow layer of the mixture into the mould and leave in the refrigerator for 1–2 hours, or until it is set. Then pour a very thin layer of the mixture on top and arrange a fan of sliced peaches on the jelly. Return to the refrigerator briefly until the peaches are held in place. Add another layer of jelly (thicker this time) and set another layer of peaches in place. Repeat until you've used all the mixture.

ALCOHOL INFUSIONS

Everyone loves sweets. When Saddam Hussein was captured in 2003, he was found with $750,000, a chicken and two Bounty Bars stashed in his refrigerator. We have a lot of fun turning popular sweets into smashing jellies using an alcohol solvent to extract the flavour.

Alcohol is an excellent solvent for volatile aromatic molecules. It does a good job of extracting and holding onto flavour from solid ingredients, ranging from herbs and fruits to nuts, spices and flowers. Leave anything in alcohol long enough, and it will extract the flavour. You can even do Mars Bars.

When you are starting out, it makes sense to use vodka as the solvent. It has little flavour of its own, so your extracts will be purer. As you are filling the vodka chockfull of the flavours and colours of your choice, buy the cheapest vodka available. You may get marginally better results from premium spirits, but you'll pay a vastly increased price to do so.

BUBBLEGUM VODKA JELLY

In the United States, 'molecular mixologist' Eban Freeman makes a bubblegum cocktail by infusing vodka with Bazooka Joe Bubble Gum. It's pretty saccharine sweet. Here in the U.K., we use indigenous Anglo Bubbly to infuse vodka to make a lurid pink, bubblegum jelly. Its artificial pear flavour will prompt anyone that eats it to reminisce at length.

FOR THE INFUSION

Unwrap the bubblegum and chop into small pieces the size of your little finger nail. Then submerge it in the vodka and leave in a covered container for 48 hours, shaking occasionally. The original vodka bottle makes a handy container if nothing else is to hand.

Strain the mixture through coffee filter paper to remove the 'crud'. You will be left with an acid-pink vodka, flavoured with bubblegum. This can be kept in a sealed container indefinitely.

FOR THE JELLY

Place the Anglo Bubbly vodka in a measuring jug and add the lemon juice, lime juice, syrup and water. You can adjust the proportions to taste, but make sure that you end up with 500ml/18fl oz of liquid.

Cut the leaf gelatine into a heatproof bowl and add enough of the vodka mixture to cover. Let the gelatine soften for 10 minutes.

Bring a pan of water to the boil and place the bowl of soft gelatine on top of the pan of boiling water. Once the gelatine has melted, add a little more vodka mixture to the bowl. Give it a stir and then pour the entire contents through a sieve and into a bowl.

Set the bowl over a larger bowl filled with iced water and add the egg whites to the jelly. Using an electric beater, whisk the mixture until there is a layer of foam on top. Pour immediately into eight glasses and place in the refrigerator to set.

For the infusion
(to extract the flavour)

10 PIECES OF ANGLO BUBBLY BUBBLEGUM

250ML/9FL OZ VODKA

For the Bubblegum Jelly
FOR 500ML/18FL OZ, ENOUGH FOR 8

200ML/7FL OZ BUBBLEGUM-INFUSED VODKA

JUICE OF ½ LEMON

JUICE OF ½ LIME

50ML/2FL OZ SUGAR SYRUP (P.29)

200ML/7FL OZ WATER

4 LEAVES OF GELATINE

3 EGG WHITES

STRIPED SKITTLES JELLY

The bubblegum technique works wonders on Skittles too. A good look is creating five infused vodkas, each one from different coloured Skittles. You can make five individual jellies, or layer them in one tin to create Neapolitan-style rainbow slices, as described below.

For the Skittles Infusions

4 PACKS OF SKITTLES

750ML/1¼ PINTS VODKA

For the Jellies

FOR 1 LITRE/1¾ PINTS,

SERVES 16

SKITTLES-INFUSED VODKA

1 LIME

250ML/9FL OZ WATER

SUGAR SYRUP (P.29), TO TASTE

10 LEAVES OF GELATINE

FOR THE INFUSIONS

Start by finding five small containers with tight-fitting lids that will each hold 150ml/5fl oz of liquid. A tupperware set could do the trick.

Open the packs of Skittles and separate out the colours into the five containers. Then pour over each one 150ml/5fl oz of vodka. Seal the containers and leave for 48 hours, shaking occasionally.

Strain the flavoured vodka through coffee filter paper into five large glasses.

FOR THE JELLY

For each coloured jelly, place 100ml/3½fl oz of Skittle vodka in a measuring jug, add a squeeze of lime juice, 50ml/2fl oz of water, and syrup to taste. If you like it sour, add more lime juice. If you like it sweet, add more syrup. Make sure you end up with 200ml/7fl oz of liquid.

Cut 2 leaves of gelatine into a heatproof bowl and add enough of this mixture to cover. Leave the gelatine to soften whilst you bring a pan of water to the boil. Place the bowl of softened gelatine on top of the pan of boiling water.

Once the gelatine has melted, add some of the vodka mixture to the bowl. Stir and then pour the whole lot through a sieve back into the jug.

You can effectively make all of the jellies at the same time if you have enough bowls. Just put them one at time over the boiling water.

To make a multi-coloured jelly, pour one of the jellies into a loaf tin and place in the refrigerator to set. Once set, continue adding layers in the same way. To serve, unmould the jelly and, using a knife dipped in hot water, carefully cut slices crossways.

LAVENDER JELLY

This jelly is a tart fella and uses a gin base to extract the lavender flavour. It's based on a recipe for the gin gimlet cocktail.

FOR THE INFUSION

Break the lavender up and submerge in the gin in a covered container for 48 hours, shaking occasionally. Strain the mixture through a fine wire sieve to remove the pieces.

FOR THE LAVENDER JELLY

Place the gin, lime juice, syrup and water in a jug.

Cut the leaf gelatine into a heatproof bowl and add enough of the gin mixture to cover. Leave the gelatine to soften for 10 minutes. Bring a pan of water to the boil and once the gelatine has softened, place the heatproof bowl on top of the pan of boiling water.

Once the gelatine has melted, add the rest of the mixture to the bowl. Stir and then pour the entire contents through a sieve into the measuring jug.

Pour this mixture into a mould and place in the refrigerator to set.

For the infusion
(to extract the flavour)

20G/¾OZ FRESH LAVENDER

250ML/9FL OZ GIN

For the Lavender Jelly
SERVES 8

250ML/9FL OZ LAVENDER-INFUSED GIN

125ML/4FL OZ FRESHLY SQUEEZED LIME JUICE

70ML/2¼FL OZ SUGAR SYRUP (P.29)

55ML/2FL OZ WATER

5 LEAVES OF GELATINE

FUTURIST BANQUET

The Futurists were utterly wild and totally ahead of their time. They were banging on about multi-sensory dining experiences decades before it was fashionable. Their *Futurist Cookbook* written in 1932 contains not only 'recipes' and manifestos but also some unreal descriptions of banquets. We particularly like the airplane banquet, where the main course of 'pork fuselage' arrives to a symphony of real airplane engines firing up.

For the 100th anniversary of Futurism in 2009, we worked with the Olde Bell to create our own aero-banquet. Over the course of the meal guests had their coats transformed into cocktails, experienced a plane crash and were served jelly out of the back of an ambulance amidst the blazing wreckage.

CAMPARI & ORANGE JELLY BOMBE

For the Campari Jelly

THIS RECIPE MAKES 500ML/18FL OZ,
BUT ADJUST THE QUANTITIES
AS NECESSARY

5 LEAVES OF GELATINE

100ML/3½ FL OZ CAMPARI

200ML/7FL OZ SUGAR SYRUP (P.29)

200ML/7FL OZ SODA WATER

PLUS 1 QUANTITY OF
ORANGE JELLY (P.34)

We developed this recipe when we were lucky enough to be asked to make the pudding for a Futurist Banquet held in New York. This recipe is our take on the Futurist Bombe. Bombes, usually ice-cream based, have a hidden inner core of a different flavour. We made a jelly bombe by creating a mould within a mould. The results are spectacular and easily replicable at home. The outer layer is a bright Campari red and the inner layer is an opaque orange jelly. It will astound your guests.

You will need two moulds, one to fit inside the other. We made a special two-part mould for ourselves, but you can make an impromptu bombe mould with a set of Tupperware bowls. You need two bowls, one with a diameter about 40mm/1½in smaller than the other. Best to read through the technique below to get familiar with the process before embarking on making this one.

WORKING OUT VOLUMES

Use a measuring jug to work out the volumes of the large and the small moulds. Then subtract one from the other to give you the volume of Campari jelly required to fill the gap between the larger and smaller moulds. Write down the volume of the smaller mould – and keep your note safe!

PREPARING THE TWO-PART MOULD

Place the large bowl on a small tray and then use a couple of rulers to suspend the smaller bowl over the larger. Now fill the small bowl with something heavy: coins, baking beans, rice … This will stop it floating away when you pour in the jelly.

CONTINUES OVERLEAF >

CAMPARI JELLY

Chop the gelatine into a heatproof bowl. Mix up the liquids and pour a little over the gelatine. When the gelatine has softened place the bowl over a pan of boiling water and allow the gelatine to melt.

Pour the rest of the Campari mixture into the bowl, stir and pour through a sieve back into a jug. To make it set a little quicker, you can stir the mixture over ice until it thickens.

Pour the jelly into the gap between the larger and smaller moulds. Allow this to set completely – about 3 hours.

ORANGE JELLY

Use the recipe for Orange Jelly on p.34 to make up the correct volume of jelly. You can do this whilst the Campari Jelly is setting and leave it out of the refrigerator until required. If it starts to solidify, melt it by placing the jug in a pan of lukewarm water and stirring occasionally.

REMOVING THE INNER MOULD AND CASTING
THE ORANGE JELLY

Once the Campari jelly has set, carefully tip out the content of the inner mould and fill it with warm water. Wait for about 20 seconds, then pull out the inner mould. It might help to twist it as you pull because there will be a fair bit of suction. You will be left with a hollow that can now be filled with the orange jelly. Fill it right up flush with the top of the Campari jelly. Carefully place in the refrigerator until fully set.

UNMOULDING

Unmould the jelly by dipping the large bowl into warm water and inverting. Serve with slices of orange.

Jelly
Cocktails

Anything liquid can be made into a jelly. As such, cocktails provide a galaxy of inspiration. If you go into a bar and like what you are drinking, turn it into a jelly. Just make your concoction, add some gelatine and refrigerate. The results can be spectacular.

The inspiration goes both ways. Barmen are taking their inspiration from chefs and turning cocktails into jellies. It's big fad at the moment, though the barmen have a habit of calling these jellies 'solids'. This is disgusting and should be stopped right away; the word has foul associations.

In this section, we'll show you how to turn a few simple cocktails into jelly. Once you have mastered these, you'll be able to turn any cocktail into a jelly.

Mai Tai

As jellies have a strong visual component, let's start off by looking at how a Mai Tai can be turned into a jelly.

The Mai Tai is a rum-based cocktail associated with Tiki culture. It's a potent drink, so as a jelly it should be treated with respect. Having said that, the Tiki styling associated with the Mai Tai is enormously silly. The drink was initially served in outlandishly decorated bars stuffed full of imitation stone heads, bamboo DJ booths and alligators strapped to the ceiling. See overleaf for some ideas for attempting your own Tiki styling.

'Trader Vic' Bergeron claims the laurels for the drink's invention. There's been some dispute about who really came up with the concoction, but this apparently 'makes his ulcer burn', so let's give Vic credit. Whatever the case, the cocktail was popularized through his global chain of high-kitsch concept bars. They still peddle the stuff today.

Be warned: this jelly will get you bongoed.

Combine the rum, curacao, orgeat syrup, sugar syrup and lime juice in a jug as if you were about to make a Mai Tai cocktail.

Cut the leaf gelatine into a heatproof bowl and add enough of this mixture to cover. Leave the gelatine to soften for 10 minutes. Bring a pan of water to the boil and, once the gelatine has softened, place the heatproof bowl on top of the pan of boiling water.

Once the gelatine has totally melted, add some of the rest of the mixture to the bowl. Stir and then pour the whole through a sieve and into the jug.

Pour this mixture into a mould or glasses and set it in the refrigerator.

When you are ready to serve, unmould and garnish with the sprig of mint.

Mai Tai – based on the original Trader Vic Formula (1944)

SERVES 4

300ML/½ PINT MEDIUM JAMAICAN RUM

75ML/5 TBSP ORANGE CURACAO

75ML/5 TBSP ORGEAT SYRUP

50ML/2FL OZ SUGAR SYRUP (P.29)

50ML/2FL OZ LIME JUICE

5 LEAVES OF GELATINE

SPRIG OF FRESH MINT, TO GARNISH

Making your Front Room into a Tiki Den

As Mai Tais are served in outlandishly decorated bars, some of the flavour will come from the setting. A paper published in 2003 by Professor John Edwards found that the same dish, *chicken à la king*, tasted different depending on the environment where it was eaten. The dish was tasted in schools, residential homes and swanky restaurants. The better the environment, the better the dish tasted. By extension, the more exotic the location you serve your Mai Tai jelly in, the more exotic it will taste. Just remember that history lesson we gave you earlier about banqueting houses – there was a reason for designing buildings just to house puddings.

SAM'S TIP FOR HOW TO TURN YOUR FRONT ROOM INTO A TIKI DEN:

A good place to start is Cheeky Tiki (www.cheekytiki.com): here you can load up on Samoan war clubs, porcupine fish and hand carved tikis. If your budget doesn't stretch to this, you'll have to go down to the garden centre and buy a load of bamboo. Split it and stick it to every surface and all over the furniture in your front room. When you have done this, you can welcome your friends to your Tiki den. Watch their jaws drop!

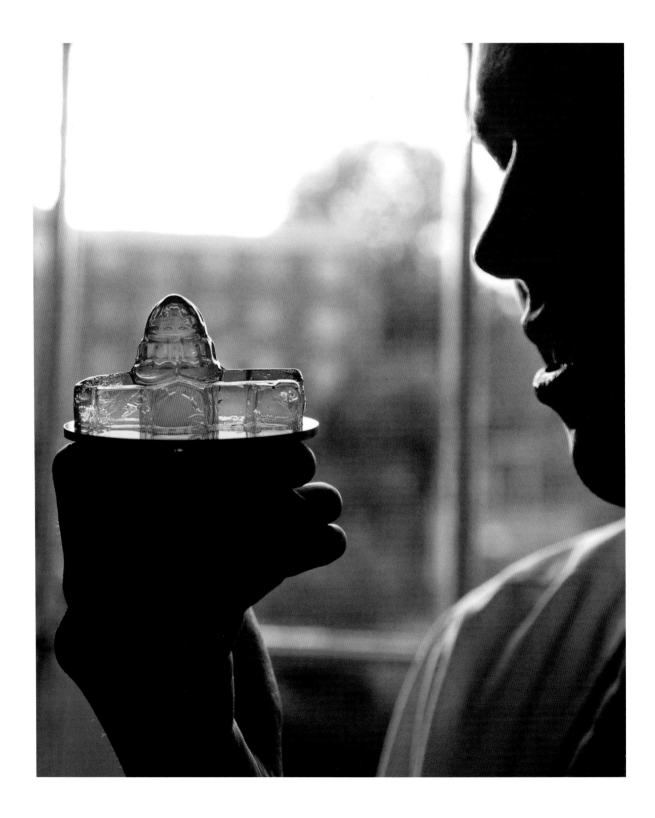

PIMM'S CUP

This is a good summer jelly for displaying your prowess at setting fruit. Alternatively, omit the fruit and make a delicious plain jelly, as we made for the picture.

Combine the Pimm's, lemonade and ginger ale in a jug as if you were about to make a jug of Pimm's. Squeeze in the lemon juice.

Cut the leaf gelatine into a heatproof bowl and add enough of this mixture to cover. Leave the gelatine to soften for 10 minutes. Bring a pan of water to the boil and place the bowl of softened gelatine on top.

Once the gelatine has totally melted, add the rest of the mixture to the bowl. Stir and then pour the whole lot through a sieve into the jug.

Pour a shallow layer of the mixture into your mould and add a layer of fruit and/or cucumber. Put the mould in the refrigerator for the jelly to set. Once set, repeat this until you've used up all the mixture.

When you are ready to serve, unmould and garnish with the sprig of mint.

SERVES 4

150ML/5FL OZ PIMM'S

175ML/6FL OZ LEMONADE

175ML/6FL OZ GINGER ALE

A SQUEEZE OF LEMON

5 LEAVES OF GELATINE

100G/3½ OZ ASSORTED FRUIT — TAKE WHAT YOU CAN GET!

CHOPPED CUCUMBER

FRESH MINT TO GARNISH

Sex on the Beach jelly

Roll up the sleeves of your pastel jacket! Snap on your Wayfarers! Here's a jelly to spirit you instantly to a yacht off the Florida Keys. An exotic Sex on the Beach jelly will have guests describing your hosting technique to neighbors for weeks to come. Don't forget to turn on Duran Duran's *Rio*. Here's to sunsets, seagulls and palm trees!

ENOUGH FOR 6 WOBBLY COCKTAILS

200ML/7FL OZ VODKA

100ML/3½ FL OZ PEACH SCHNAPPS

200ML/7FL OZ CRANBERRY JUICE

200ML/7FL OZ ORANGE JUICE

5 LEAVES OF GELATINE

FLESH OF 2 ORANGES

6 MARTINI GLASSES

6 COCKTAIL UMBRELLAS

GLACÉ CHERRIES

In a jug, combine the vodka, schnapps, cranberry juice and orange juice.

Cut up the gelatine into thumb-size pieces and place in a heatproof bowl. Pour over enough of the mix to cover and allow to soften for 10 minutes.

Meanwhile, bring a small pan of water to a simmer. Place the bowl of softened gelatine on top of the simmering water and stir occasionally until dissolved. This will take about 10 minutes.

While you are waiting, dice the orange flesh and divide between the cocktail glasses. Once the gelatine has entirely melted, combine with the remainder of the cocktail mixture and pour through a sieve into the glasses. Refrigerate to set.

Garnish with the cocktail umbrellas and some lurid glacé cherries before serving.

WEIRD & WONDERFUL

FUNERAL JELLY

This jelly is our take on funeral cakes, a long forgotten element of the funeral ceremony. In the past, funeral cakes – which were much like shortbread – were served with a glass of ale or Madeira after the interment. Two female 'servers' distributed the cakes, and it was these women who walked at the head of the funeral procession. The cakes were traditionally wrapped in black crêpe paper and moulded to depict motifs such as skulls, hearts and roses.

We initially became interested in funeral cakes because they are a prime example of a moulded food as well as being thrillingly macabre. Original funeral moulds were made in metal, wood and ceramic, and motifs included the three plumes that decorate hearses; roosters, symbolizing resurrection; and Masonic symbols.

After a bit of research, we let things lie until we were asked to make a jelly for someone's funeral! Wow! It seemed like a good opportunity to revive the custom of funeral cakes but in a magical jellied format. In retrospect, it makes sense. We produce vast amounts of jellies for jaded wedding guests, so it's understandable that grieving families want in on the action. After all, funerals and weddings are both celebrations of life.

The trick was to create a recipe and design a mould that were both in keeping with the tone of the ceremony. We settled on a simple pyramid mould, referencing the grandest tombs of all time. A black cherry and prosecco jelly complimented the sombre yet celebratory occasion, and is lent extra panache by the 24-carat-gold tip.

After debuting the funeral jelly at the private event, we looked for an opportunity to launch a funeral jelly service to the general public. One presented itself with the global wave of grief around Michael Jackson's death. London restaurant Bistrotheque boldly put the jelly on the menu for the day of Michael Jackson's funeral, and diners were served quivering pyramids by waiters wearing a single white glove.

Black cherry &
Prosecco funeral jelly

It is hoped that the Funeral Jelly will act as powerful *memento mori* to inspire eaters to live life to the full. At the end of some Egyptian feasts, a small model of a mummified corpse was passed round before wine was served, to prompt the feasters to seize the day. *Carpe diem!*

FOR 10 SMALL JELLIES

FOR THE GOLDEN TIPS,
SEE PAGES 74—75.

400G/14OZ BLACK CHERRIES

50G/1¾ OZ CASTER SUGAR

350ML/12FL OZ PROSECCO

JUICE OF ½ LEMON

5 LEAVES OF GELATINE

Begin by making your golden tips (see instructions on pp.74—75). Ensure they have time to fully set whilst you embark on the rest of the recipe.

Start by adding the black cherries to a small saucepan with the sugar and 100ml/3½fl oz of the prosecco. Cook covered over a low heat until the cherries are totally tender — up to 45 minutes. Pass the softened cherries and juice through a sieve lined with a tea towel. Let gravity do the work — we want the cherry juice to be extra smooth.

Once the black cherry juice has run through, combine it in a measuring jug with the rest of the prosecco and lemon juice. You need 500ml/18fl oz of liquid, so top up with prosecco if necessary.

Use some of this liquid to cover your chopped gelatine in a bowl. Allow the gelatine to soften for 5 minutes. Bring a pan of water to the boil and place the bowl of softened gelatine on top of the pan. Once the gelatine has melted, add half of the measuring jug mixture at the last minute, then strain the gelatine mixture back into the jug, stirring all the time.

Now you are ready to pour the black cherry jelly mixture into the mould on top of the gold layer. Before you do so, make sure the gold layer is fully set. It's worth making sure that the cherry mix has cooled to room temperature too. If it is poured hot, you run the risk of melting some of the gold mixture, and gold leaf will float around the rest of the jelly — which won't look at all smart. Lower the temperature by stirring the mixture over ice. Alternatively, pour the jelly out onto a tray and the temperature will drop rapidly.

Finish setting the jelly in the refrigerator for a couple of hours.

HIPPOCRAS

There is real scope to bring back the jelly as a Christmas dessert and alternative to heavy Christmas puddings. Stomachs need to be respected – indeed, the Victorians often referred to them as amiable gentlemen – and a light jelly makes a much more manageable dessert. We'll demonstrate that you can ditch the Christmas pudding but lose none of the traditions.

For this jelly, we use a recipe once enjoyed by Henry VIII and which the notorious serial killer Gilles de Rais called 'Jelly Hippocras'. Hippocras is a medieval drink that is similar to mulled wine, infused with spices and sugar, but it was invariably served at room temperature. As with traditional Christmas pudding, it's important that 13 ingredients are used to represent Jesus and his disciples. Interestingly, Christmas puddings were banned by the Puritans in 1664 for being lewd. If they had seen the wobble on this Christmas pudding, they'd have been even more shocked.

The golden age of jelly and the origins of modern Christmas both come from the same period: the Victorians are responsible for both. Christmas trees were not popularized until 1848, when the Royal Family were pictured standing in front of one. At this time, jelly was considered a fine centrepiece and was often laid along the table for the entirety of the meal.

Sadly, jellies no longer take centre stage at Christmas, though they continue to play important supporting roles. We're all familiar with cranberry and redcurrant jelly. And jams and preserves, close relatives to jellies, come in to their own at this time of year, when fresh fruit is in short supply.

The Victorians set lots of small keepsakes within their Christmas puddings, which were used to foretell the future. If you set items in the jelly, you can do the same. If you discover a ring, legend has it the next year will bring true love; coins bring wealth; and thimbles are the booby prize. If you get a thimble in your pudding, you'll remain single forever!

CONTINUES OVERLEAF >

JOLLY OLD CHRISTMAS.

HIPPOCRAS CHRISTMAS PUDDING JELLY

Hippocras improves with resting, but if you don't tend to plan meals a month in advance it will still be just fine. This recipe gives you more than you will need for a Christmas pudding for four, so you can serve the rest at drinks parties around the festive period.

All you have to do is add all the ingredients to a large stock pot and heat gently for 1 hour. At this point, it can be strained and stored in sterilized bottles as necessary. Traditionally, the wine would steep in the spices for a week or more before being strained.

TO MAKE THE CHRISTMAS PUDDING JELLY

Cut the leaf gelatine into a heatproof bowl with a pair of scissors. Add 100ml/3½fl oz of hippocras to cover the gelatine.

Leave the gelatine to soften for 10 minutes. Bring a pan of water to the boil and place the bowl of softened gelatine on top of the pan. Once the gelatine has totally melted, add the rest of the hippocras to the mixture before passing the lot through a sieve and back into a bowl.

Place the bowl with the cooling jelly over a larger bowl filled with ice. Now stir until the mixture starts to thicken. At this point, you can add the raisins, candied peel and metal! You need to stir the jelly to the point that you can get all your objects evenly distributed but not so much that the jelly is excessively lumpy. It still has to be able to fill all the contours of your mould (or pudding basin). When the jelly is just right, encourage it into a mould and place in the refrigerator to finish setting.

All that's left now is to unmould the jelly and discover who is going to be unlucky in love for the rest of their life. If you're going all-out, garnish the jelly with holly and pour over 1 tablespoon of rum before igniting it.

Happy Christmas!

For the Hippocras

3 BOTTLES RED WINE

200G/7OZ CASTER SUGAR

1 CINNAMON STICK

2 TSP GROUND GINGER

1 TSP GRATED NUTMEG

1 TSP CLOVES

1 TSP CRUSHED CARDAMOM SEEDS

For the Jelly

5 LEAVES OF GELATINE

500ML/18FL OZ HIPPOCRAS

2 TSP RAISINS

2 TSP CANDIED CITRUS PEEL

1 RING

1 SMALL COIN

1 THIMBLE

Glow in the dark jelly

With jelly, half the fun lies in the spectacle. People always enjoy the wobble, but that's to be expected. No-one is surprised by a wobbly jelly. To really bowl them over, you have to sex it up a lot. One way of doing this is to make it glow in the dark.

In the summer of 2009, we were commissioned to create the most outlandish menu imaginable to be served on a Pullman train carriage touring the country. The event was organized by Hendrick's Gin, and curious visitors were plied with fine alcohol. The most interesting visitors were invited to a banquet hosted in the carriage each evening, which they were assured would be the most peculiar meal of their life.

We wanted to use the gin as part of a jelly that took people by surprise and ambushed their senses. Weird-tasting jelly would be too obvious – and not nice! So visual trickery was the key.

The previous year we had worked with Dr Andrea Sella, an explosives expert at University College London, developing glow in the dark jellies. We decided to use the techniques developed in his laboratory for maximum impact on the carriage. The dinner guests went wild!

To make the jelly glow in the dark, food-safe quinine is included as an ingredient and the jellies are served in an area where UV blacklights cause them to fluoresce. The invisible ultraviolet light from the blacklights is absorbed by the quinine, which then re-emits bluish light at the edge of the visible spectrum, making the jellies appear to glow in the dark.

Dr Sella explains the phenomenon like this:

Fluorescence is one of those truly magical atomic phenomena – an optical illusion that makes things look brighter than they are, making it central not only to safety equipment but also to detergents and cleaning agents to give that 'whiter than white' look. All manner of materials fluoresce. The quinine molecule itself is a natural product from the bark of the South American Cinchona tree, [which] has been added to drinks for over a century. One of the first anti-malarial molecules, it began to be used by the British in India as a cure for fevers. The drug could be made more palatable by judicious addition of sugar and alcohol. Nowadays, the malaria parasite is resistant to quinine, but its bitterness adds a pleasant 'bite' to the flavour of many soft drinks and mixers. And the blue glow is a delightful effect that adds ambience to pubs and clubs. But if you don't like the glow there's a simple way to switch it off — simply toss a pinch of salt into your cocktail and kill the effect in an instant.

To be really effective, you need total darkness save for the UV light. As we were running the carriage banquets on summer nights in a train carriage with no blinds, there was a good deal of ambient light well into the evening. We hid a UV light underneath the dining table in the carriage. When it came to the dessert course, guests were encouraged to hold their plates in the relative darkness under the table to see the glow. The jellies sprang into vivid glowing colours. Most peculiar was not the glowing jelly but watching all the guests holding their plates under the table!

We have used rosewater and gin to create our glow-in-the-dark cocktail. All that remains is for you to get a UV blacklight from your local DIY store and the fun begins...

BLACK FOOD

*Don't you think it's appropriate that the most expensive items are
black?* THE COOK, THE THIEF, HIS WIFE AND HER LOVER

Black is beautiful and black food has provided the basis for some of the
most memorable literary and historic meals. In Huysman's *Against
Nature*, the hero Des Esseintes hosts a feast:

> *The dining room, draped in black, opened out onto a garden
> metamorphosed for the occasion, the paths being strewn with
> charcoal, the ornamental pond edged with black basalt and filled
> with ink, and the shrubberies replanted with cypresses and pines.
> The dinner itself was served on a black cloth adorned with
> baskets of violets and scabious; a candelabrum shed an eerie
> green light over the table and tapers flickered in the chandeliers.*

> *While a hidden orchestra played funeral marches, the guests
> were waited on by naked negresses wearing only slippers and
> stockings in cloth of silver embroiderd with tears.*

> *Dining off black-bordered plates, the company had enjoyed
> turtle soup, Russian rye bread, ripe olives from Turkey, caviar,
> mullet botargo, black puddings from Frankfurt, game served in
> sauce the colour of liquorices and boot-polish, truffle jellies,
> chocolate creams, plum-puddings, nectarines, pears in grape-
> juice syrup, mulberries, and black-heart cherries. From
> dark-tinted glasses they had drunk the wines of Limagne and
> Roussillon, of Tenedos, Valdepenas, and Oporto. And after coffee
> and walnut cordial, they had rounded off the evening with kvass,
> porter and stout.*

> *On the invitations, which were similar to those sent out before
> more solemn obsequies, this dinner was described as a funeral
> banquet in memory of the host's virility, lately but only
> temporarily deceased.*

This literary meal was based on an earlier banquet that caused a scandal in Parisian high society. In 1783, Grimod de La Reynière, seen by many as the first restaurant critic, hosted a black banquet with invitations so extraordinary that Louis XVI is said to have acquired one to frame. Bordered in black to resemble funeral notices, these were sent to 300 guests, although only 22 were to dine: following the protocol of the time, the rest were to observe the festivities.

There's also a well-documented Renaissance black, or hell, banquet hosted in 1511 by dining group The Company of the Trowel. On arrival, guests were invited by Pluto to join him in the Underworld for his wedding feast to Proserpina. Entering through the gaping mouth of Hades, which was hinged to open and close for each couple in turn, guests found themselves in a circular room gloomily lit by one small candle. A hideous devil with pitchfork showed them to their places at a black draped table, while their host declaimed that the torments of Hell would be suspended for the time being in honor of his wedding. About the walls of the room were pictured the 'holes' of the damned, their varying tortures periodically revealed by 'flames' that flared up beneath them.

The food served seemed repulsive — serpents, lizards, toads, newts, spiders, frogs, scorpions and the like. Inside these deceptive exteriors, though, delicious tidbits were hidden. The dishes were served on a fire shovel, while wine was poured by a 'devil' from a rhyton, a drinking vessel in the shape of an animal's head. Skeleton bones made of sugar and marzipan formed the dessert course.

This weight of precedent is inspirational. We teamed up with party planner Fiona Leahy and Michael Cirino of *a razor, a shiny knife* to create our own monochromatic meal. Michael Cirino created an eight-course meal, where all the dishes were black; we built black liquorice jelly ziggurats; and Fiona Leahy created the most spectacular setting.

LIQUORICE JELLY

You can buy liquorice sticks from health food stores. The sticks are very brittle and, arguably, inedible. However, when soaked they render an unbelievably sweet and dark liquorice water. It is this liquorice water that is going to be used to flavour the jelly.

Break the liquorice up into pieces 1cm/½ in long and place in a measuring jug. Add about 150ml/5fl oz of water, or certainly enough so that the sticks are covered. Stir with a fork from time to time. It will take about 2 hours for the liquorice to dissolve. To speed up the process, you can chop the sticks up smaller to begin with.

The liquid will now be a deep black colour, highly flavoured and very sweet. Liquorice contains a naturally occurring sweetener called glycyrrhizin, which can be 50 times sweeter than sugar, so you don't need to add any sugar to the jelly.

Add water to the liquorice water until you have 500ml/18fl oz. If it tastes too sweet or strong then dilute it to taste and pour away any excess.

Cut the leaves of gelatine into a few pieces and place in a heatproof bowl. Add a few tablespoons of the jelly mixture so that the gelatine is just covered. Let the gelatine soften for 10 minutes whilst you bring a small pan of water to a simmer. Place the bowl of softened gelatine over the simmering water and leave until totally melted. Add the remainder of the jelly mixture to the melted gelatine and stir to combine.

Pour through a sieve into a jug and then carefully fill your mould. Refrigerate until set.

1 STICK OF LIQUORICE

150ML/5FL OZ WATER

5 LEAVES OF GELATINE

BACON COLA JELLIES

Fat-washing may sound disgusting. But it does let you infuse various liquids with the flavour of melted fat – and if done properly does not leave a greasy taste or texture. Some of the top bars and restaurants are using the technique to create unusual beverages like buttered rums. And we use it to make Bacon Cola Jelly. You can use the technique to impress your friends and scare vegetarians.

As you are using a fizzy drink in this jelly, there is a technique developed by Len Fisher and used by Heston Blumenthal to make the jelly extra fizzy. The trick is to cool the jelly rapidly and to ensure that the cola is at its fizziest when added to the mix.

BACON VODKA

For the Fat-washed Vodka

6 RASHERS OF SMOKY BACON

200ML/7FL OZ VODKA

For the Jelly

5 LEAVES OF GELATINE

200ML/7FL OZ BACON VODKA

SQUEEZE OF LEMON

300ML/10FL OZ CHILLED COLA

Fry the bacon and let it cool on kitchen paper, then add it to the vodka in a sealed plastic container. Place the container in a dark cupboard for about 2 weeks, or until you get bored. Move the container to the freezer. The fat will freeze, but the vodka will not. Filter the bacon vodka through coffee filters. This will keep indefinitely.

EXTRA FIZZY JELLIES

Place four glasses in the freezer to cool down.

Cut the leaf gelatine into a heatproof bowl and add half the bacon vodka. Leave the gelatine to soften for 10 minutes. Add the lemon juice.

Bring a pan of water to the boil and place the bowl of gelatine on top. Once the gelatine has melted, add the remainder of the bacon vodka and stir. Sieve into a jug. Divide equally between the four frozen glasses.

Open the cola and quick as a flash divide this between the four glasses. Place all the glasses back in the freezer for 20 minutes – and no longer; it's important that your jelly does not freeze, or it will be ruined.

Transfer the jellies to the refrigerator to set for around 6 hours. Using this technique will make for super-fizzy jellies.

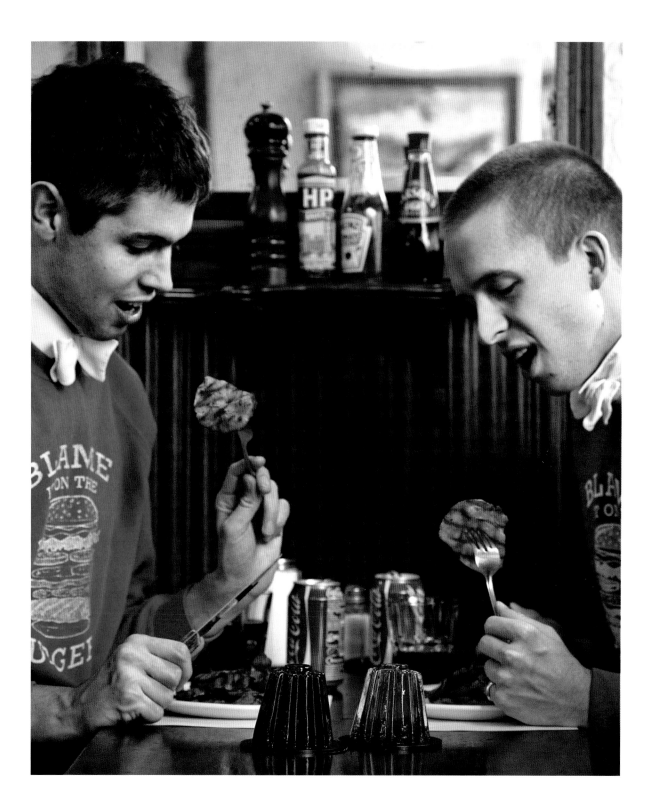

FLAMING JELLY

This is less of a recipe and more of an instructional. You can turn any jelly into a flaming jelly!

We looked at loads of different ways of doing this, using some full-on chemicals and speaking to some top scientists. The methods we developed using complex setting techniques and some strange chemicals work pretty effectively. What works even more effectively, though, is the simplest method: pour over-proof spirit over your jelly and torch it. The more potent the spirit, the better it will burn. When Sam does this, he uses a 151% proof spirit. Alcohol burns with a low temperature flame, so the jelly won't melt too much before the alcohol burns off and the flames die down.

Weirdly, the less explanation you give, the more people will think you are doing something terribly clever. Some aspects of cooking are a bit like doing a magic trick. When you know how it's done, it seems obvious and tired. When you don't know the method, it appears to be a miracle.

The most memorable time setting fire to jelly was at the Oxford Symposium on Food and Cookery. Sam and his brother created a banquet table for a Samuel Pepys memorial meal cooked by Fergus Henderson. They made the Great Fire of London in jelly with a huge centrepiece of the old St Paul's Cathedral surrounded by hundreds of jelly houses. When the diners had gathered, the jelly was spectacularly set alight. Sam's brother was holding a large burning tray of jelly and was getting seriously scorched. But every time he cried out for someone to bring a towel to beat out the flames, the crowd cheered more – they thought it was part of the act! He managed to style it out in the end, but the situation was pretty intense.

APHRODISIAC JELLY

The best way to get someone into bed is to touch their most sensitive organ; the belly!

Over the course of history, pretty much every vaguely exotic ingredient has been seen as an aphrodisiac. Vanilla, oysters and bananas all look rude, and have been credited with mysterious powers of arousal. There's little to substantiate their claims.

What works is extravagance and alcohol. If the food looks and tastes expensive and combines a knockout punch, you're getting there. Flowers also help. This recipe sexes-up our wedding jelly formula to make it go with a bang. When we served it at the School of Life's Sunday morning sermon on seduction, one man exposed himself. We're not sure how seductive this was, but it goes to show that the recipe makes an impact.

The diethyl ether is optional, but will give an extra-intoxicating kick.

CHAMPAGNE, ROSE & STRAWBERRY JELLY

Use 1 leaf of gelatine, the gold and 3½ tablespoons of the Champagne to make a gold and Champagne suspension, following the technique on pp.74–75. Set this as the first layer of your jelly in the mould.

Meanwhile, cut the rest of the leaf gelatine into a heatproof bowl with a pair of scissors. Add enough Champagne to cover (about 100ml/3½fl oz). Leave the gelatine to soften for 10 minutes.

Bring a pan of water to the boil and place the bowl of softened gelatine on top of the pan of boiling water. Once the gelatine has totally melted, stir in the sugar until it has dissolved and add another 100ml/3½fl oz of Champagne to the mixture.

Combine the melted gelatine mixture with the rest of the Champagne by pouring it through a sieve and into a measuring jug; this will also remove any unmelted lumps. Add the rose essence and diethyl ether to the mixture. Squeeze the lemon through the sieve too. Top up with Champagne until you have 500ml/18fl oz.

Place the washed fruit into the bottom of the mould and pour in about one-third of the jelly. Put the mould in the refrigerator for the jelly to set. Leave until set enough so that the fruit seems safely embedded (about 2 hours), then pour over the rest of the jelly mixture and return to the refrigerator.

If you don't want to set the fruit in the mould first, simply add everything to the mould at once. Doing a double set, however, makes sure that the fruit floats elegantly in the unmoulded jelly rather than sinking to the bottom.

FOR 500ML/17FL OZ. SERVES 4

5 LEAVES OF GELATINE

5 LEAVES OF GOLD LEAF

450ML/16FL OZ CHAMPAGNE OR SPARKLING WINE

40G/1½OZ CASTER SUGAR

8 DROPS OF DIETHYL ETHER

4 TSP ROSE ESSENCE

A SQUEEZE OF LEMON JUICE

A FEW STRAWBERRIES

Sun-Coffee Jelly
(with optional cigarettes!)

You can make this jelly using coffee in the regular way, but it won't have the same pizzazz. Sun-infusing coffee or tea brings out a completely different flavour profile. Most importantly, more caffeine is extracted, which means you can make a jelly that's like rocket fuel.

FOR THE INFUSION

For the Infusion

500ML/18FL OZ WATER

100ML/3½FL OZ DARK ROASTED COFFEE AT A COARSE GRIND

1 SMALL CINNAMON STICK

Sam likes to use a dark roasted coffee, as it has a stronger flavour profile, which means the coffee taste transfers more effectively. You also get a richer colour.

Place the water and coffee in a transparent and sealable glass jar, then give it a shake. Put the jar outside where the sun will strike it and try to shake vigorously every now and again. Leave for 2–3 days. Remove the cinnamon stick and then pour through coffee filter paper to remove the grinds.

FOR THE JELLY

For the Jelly

450ML/16FL OZ SUN-INFUSED COFFEE

50ML/2FL OZ SUGAR SYRUP (P.29)

1 DROP VANILLA ESSENCE

5 LEAVES OF GELATINE

Combine the sun-infused coffee, sugar syrup and vanilla essence in a jug.

Cut the leaf gelatine into a heatproof bowl and add enough of the coffee mixture to cover. Leave the gelatine to soften for 10 minutes. Bring a pan of water to the boil and place the bowl of softened gelatine on top of the pan.

Once the gelatine has totally melted, add some of the remaining mixture to the bowl. Stir and then pour the whole lot through a sieve into the jug.

Pour this mixture into a mould and place in the refrigerator to set.

CIGARETTE BONUS BOX

If you want to turn the jelly into a killer morning snack, why not concoct a tobacco syrup to add to the recipe? Beware: the tobacco syrup will make the jelly tasty, but it could give you cancer!

We suggest using a tobacco with lots of flavour to make the syrup. Black Cavendish is good; it has a fine vanilla note that sets off the coffee (see Suppliers, p.157). Otherwise, crumble a favourite cigar for the syrup.

FOR THE TOBACCO SYRUP

50ML/2FL OZ WATER

50G/1¾ OZ CASTER SUGAR

1 TBSP GOOD TOBACCO

Combine the water and sugar in a pan. Stir and heat until all the sugar has dissolved.

Turn the heat off and bang the tobacco in. Leave it to steep for 30 seconds, then pour through a sieve to remove the tobacco leaves.

FOR THE JELLY

Follow the recipe for the Sun Coffee Jelly opposite but replace the normal sugar syrup with your tobacco syrup.

Appendix

GELLING AGENTS

There are better things to do in life than read a chapter about gels. But if you are really interested, here's what we know:

GELATINE

Gelatine is the ultimate gelling agent. Gelatine jellies are wonderful to look at, glisten beautifully and have a marvelous wobble. They have a suppleness and texture that make gelatine jellies a joy to eat. The melting point is below body temperature, which means they melt in the mouth.

You will need to come to terms with the fact that gelatine is derived from animals. In Europe and the United States, gelatine is mostly derived from pigskin, though it is sometimes made from cowskin or from bone. This does seem a bit brutal but we like to think that these by-products of industrial meat production would go to waste if they weren't turned into fine jellies.

Now for the chemistry bit. Gelatine comes from the collagen proteins extracted (via acid baths) from animal skin. When heated, the collagen's triple helix structure uncoils and dissolves in the water. As it cools below the melting temperature of gelatine (around body temperature), the collagen naturally tries to re-organize itself into its original triple helix. However, it does not attain this original structure because adjacent collagen helixes randomly bind to each other to form a net of gelatine molecules. At a concentration of about 1%, this net traps the liquid in its interstices, stopping movement and turning the solution into a gel. If you want even more of this sort of thing look at *McGee on Food and Cooking* or the *Big Fat Duck Cookbook*: they're our first port of call when we need to get scientific!

Using higher concentrations of gelatine will give you a stronger jelly. It will be less fragile and won't melt as fast outside the refrigerator. On the other hand, if you have a jelly that has too high a concentration, it will wobble less and become rubbery (and will even bounce when dropped). In this book, we have calibrated the gel strength for good eating jellies.

Gelatine comes in a number of different forms. You can buy powdered gelatine and leaf gelatine in grades ranging from bronze to platinum. We like to use high grade leaf gelatine, which gives a clearer jelly without the yellowish tinge and piggy smell of the lower grades. Lower grade gelatine and powdered gelatine is, of course, cheaper. It is useful for making jellies to look at rather than eat.

There are a number of other factors that will increase and decrease your gel strength. Adjust the concentration of gelatine accordingly:

- the longer you leave a jelly in the refrigerator, the stronger it gets

- acids, such as lemon juice, make a weaker jelly

- alcohol above 45% proof stops gelatine setting

- some fruit like kiwis and pineapples have protein-digesting enzymes that will stop a jelly setting. For instructions on how to counter this, see p.50

- milk-based jellies set firmer

- the more slowly you let the temperature of the jelly drop, the greater the gel strength (the gelatine network can organize more effectively).

A vegetarian gelling agent as good as gelatine remains the holy grail of food scientists. The person that cracks it will be rich.

Here are some non-meaty gelling agents:

AGAR AGAR

Agar agar is a vegetarian gel extracted from a number of red seaweeds. It is commonly used in the study of microbiology, but you can use it to make hot jellies. Agar is commonly used in Asia to make fruit jellies. If it's not stocked in your local supermarket, head across to a Japanese or Chinese grocery store.

To make an agar jelly, you won't need as high a concentration as with gelatine – between 0.5 % and 1.5% of the final volume of the gel. First soak the agar in cold water, then heat it to the boil to fully dissolve it. Once you have combined the agar with the other ingredients and strained the mixture to get rid of any lumps, it will set at around 38°C (100°F). You won't even need to put it in the refrigerator. After an agar gel has set, it won't remelt until it is heated beyond 85°C (185°F). You can use this property to make hot jellies. We sometimes use agar to make a hot apple crumble jelly – though it's not especially nice!

The problem with agar jellies is that they lack the glorious texture and mouthfeel of gelatine jellies. Agar jellies won't wobble as well, are more crumbly, look slightly opaque and most importantly don't melt in the mouth. Due to the higher melting point, they are also impossible to unmould.

Canny cooks can combine weak gelatine gels with agar gels to enjoy the benefits of both gelling agents. So you can get a jelly that wobbles and has a decent texture (from the gelatine) but is more stable up until you serve it (agar).

GELLAN

We've got a load of both low and high acyl gellan in the cupboard, but we've never got around to using it: we keep meaning to have a play with it but always get distracted. Apparently it allows you to make hot and firm jellies for slicing – just what we've always wanted.

CARAGEENAN

This can be used to make a vegetarian gel. Industrial jelly manufacturers use it to make the lurid 'dessert pots' that sit in the non-refrigerated section of a supermarket. As it gels at a higher temperature, it does not have to be chilled and can keep for ages unlike fresh jelly. This is an advantage for manufacturers but not for the eater! The texture is awful. The gel is flaccid but at the same time crumbles in the mouth. Also carageenan has recently been identified as a cancer risk … enjoy!

Using ceramic
& glass moulds

Not all jelly moulds are made of copper, and it's a good bet that you've got some ceramic or glass moulds knocking around. But, as many will testify, they can be impossible to unmould. As both glass and ceramic are poor conductors of heat, you can't rely on putting them in a basin of hot water to loosen the jelly: by the time the last part of the surface has melted, there's a chance that half the jelly has melted too.

Food historian Ivan Day discovered that the traditional way of using these mould was to first line them with a thin layer of tallow (mutton fat). The tallow was brushed onto the inside of the mould and the jelly carefully poured in. It was vital that the jelly was relatively cool so as not to melt the tallow. Fortunately, Ivan doesn't suggest that you track down some rendered mutton fat but instead use its modern equivalent, Trex, a vegetable shortening available in all supermarkets.

TO PREPARE THE MOULD

Use a pastry brush to apply a thin film of Trex onto the inside of the mould, making sure that you continue right up to the rim. Pour the cool jelly in and refrigerate until set.

TO UNMOULD THE JELLY

Firstly gently push down around the perimeter of the jelly using your fingers so that the jelly pulls away from the mould. Then, turning the jelly on its side, give it a good shake: if you hear it making slapping noises, you know that it is ready to be turned out. If it won't perform a rude wobble solo for you, try to get some air into the mould by carefully putting a finger between the mould and the jelly – crude but it works. It does take some practice, but the results are worth it.

If you are having difficulty unmoulding from thick-gauge plastic moulds, the above method will work wonders on them too.

EVENTS

Victorian Breakfast *Warwick Castle* December 2007

Warwick Castle commissioned us to create a full-on, twelve-course, Victorian breakfast. We got stuck into some serious research and discovered that a breakfast of similar magnitude had been served to Queen Victoria on a train. Drawing on this for inspiration, we wrote our menu.

It was huge. A single person's meal clocked in at over 4000 calories. Just one of the courses was a full English breakfast; another was a dish called scotch woodcock, basically a sexed-up version of scrambled eggs, using only yolks and double cream, and served with anchovies.

Each guest needed a battery of cutlery to get through the meal, so the table had to be re-laid three times. To add to the difficulties, the food was coming out of three separate kitchens. Harry drew up architectural drawings showing table laying and relaying, food production flows and serving choreography for each of the twelve courses. It got us through.

An edge of surrealism was added by the life size waxwork of Queen Victoria standing at the side of the dining room, and the organ music from the fairground outside.

To cement the link between jelly and architecture, we put on an Architectural Jelly Banquet in the mighty Quad of University College, London (UCL). In the run-up to the event, we created a jelly design competition, which attracted entries from some of the world's leading architects, including Rogers Stirk Harbour + Partners, Lord Foster and Will Alsop. In total, over a hundred designs were submitted from as far afield as Brazil and the United States.

For the event, we lit the buildings of UCL's Neo-Classical Quad to look like jellies and pumped the space full of the smell of strawberries. It was like stepping inside a vast jelly. Over 2000 people came to look at the jelly designs, eat jelly and party. The centrepiece was a 14m (46ft) long self-wobbling jelly table with hundreds of illuminated jellies. It looked spectacular. A waggle engine strapped to the bottom of the table created a non-stop wobbling effect.

Choreographed dancers performed with giant spoons against a soundscape by Douglas Murphey made from sampling jellies wobbling. He used UCL's anechoic chamber – a special room lined with sound absorbing materials, to record the sound of jelly wobbling. The sonic wobble was captured in two ways: by carefully recording the results of gentle coaxing and by expressing the wobble frequency as physically powerful bass tones. It sounded rude. You can listen for yourself on YouTube.

Heston Blumenthal popped down to present the prize of ultimate jelly architect to Tonkin Liu. At 11pm, the exhibition wound up and the party began with jelly wrestling and a huge food fight.

Scratch 'n' Sniff Cinema *ICA/Jotta Craft Fair* February 2009

Making Peter Greenaway's *The Cook, The Thief, His Wife and Her Lover* an even more visceral experience is a challenge. For a Valentine's Day screening, we created aromas including 'rotting meat' and 'dusty books' to capture the scent of key moments of the film. These aromas were micro-encapsulated and printed onto special scratch 'n' sniff cards given to the audience to scratch along to the production.

During an extended interval, they got stuck into a cinema food concession that had been possessed by the film. The popcorn machine held a naked body, hotdogs were enrobed with 24-carat gold, and the pick 'n' mix featured flashing boiled sweets and roll-your-own candy tobacco.

Brilliantly, we were able to corner Peter Greenaway at the ICA the week before. He kindly let us record an interview to introduce the film. While we were talking, he let slip what he would cook to seduce a woman: crocodile!

Because the printing on the scratch 'n' sniff cards was so expensive, we had to run three back-to-back screenings to break even. We were haunted by the film's soundtrack for weeks afterwards from listening to it non-stop.

So many people turned up to the final screening that we had to beg bar stools from the pub next door and borrow chairs from the offices across the road to seat everyone.

Alcoholic Architecture *Newburgh Quarter, London* April 2009

Buildings can be transformed into breathable beverages by filling them with a cocktail fog. Alcoholic Architecture saw Bompas & Parr create a walk-in cloud of breathable cocktail.

Visitors donned protective suits and stepped into a mist of vaporized gin and tonic, which they imbibed through inhaling. Doctors were our mixologists for the event, performing a complex series of calculations to calibrate the ratio of alcohol to mixer. It was important that visitors were able to walk out of the installation and not crawl out on their hands and knees!

Stepping inside the cloud was strange and disorientating. If your friend was a metre away, you weren't able to see them because there was so much Hendrick's Gin and tonic in the air between you.

Vaporizing the cocktail seemed to heighten the flavour for an ultra-intense G&T experience. Visitors from the Institute of Food Research thought that breathing in different ways let them taste the different botanicals in the gin. All the while, the alcohol was being absorbed via the lungs and even the eyeballs.

Architectural Punch Bowl *33 Portland Place, London* December 2009

For the Architectural Punch Bowl we worked with Courvoisier to explode cocktails to the grandest size – the scale of buildings. After a six month research project with UCL we flooded 33 Portland Place with over four tons of punch; enough for 25,000 people. The Punch Bowl was so large that engineers Arup had to make sure the building wouldn't collapse under the weight of alcohol. Visitors rafted across the punch before having a drink and toying with the remote control garnishes.

INDEX

SUPPLIERS

BLACK LIGHTS/ UV LIGHTS

You can buy a black light and fittings at any decent sized DIY store, or one of those shops that sells bongs, drapes and lighters that look like handguns to 11-year-old boys. If you want something with a bit more punch, try Stage Electrics for a UV cannon. Stage Electrics is a special effects treasure trove. While you're there, pick up theatrical blood and an artificial snow machine.

Stage Electrics: 0844 870 0077
www.stage-electrics.co.uk

FRUIT

If you are going to make a large amount of fruit jelly, it is worthwhile hitting up a wholesale market. We get up ridiculously early to catch the wholesale fruit and veg market at Borough. One pleasure of going this early is the local pub, which has a special market licence. As many of the traders would have been working all night, it is allowed to serve alcohol between 6 and 8.30 am!

www.boroughmarket.org.uk

GELATINE

In the baking section of any half-decent supermarket. Buy the fine leaf gelatine: Dr Oetker's gelatine is what we use the most. It's not hard to find.

GOLD

You could go to a fancy art shop for your gold. We don't. Ours is from Leyland, the builders' merchant, because it's cheaper. Further discounts are contingent on which football team you support. Make sure you buy gold over 22 carat so that it is safe to eat.

Leyland SDM: 020 7275 2999
www.leylandsdm.co.uk

Cornelissen & Son: 020 7636 1045
105 Great Russell Street,
London, WC1B 3RY

TIKI

Cheeky Tiki is the best place for Samoan war staffs and dried puffer fish. Bamboo can be found at your nearest garden center.

Cheeky Tiki: www.cheekytiki.com

TOBACCO

If you are going to cook with tobacco, use good stuff. G. Smith and Sons on the Charing Cross Road in London opened in 1869 and is where we buy ours.

G. Smith & Sons: 0207 836 7422
74 Charing Cross Road,
London, WC2H 0BG

BIBLIOGRAPHY

Archbold, Rick et al. *Last Dinner on the Titanic: Menus and Recipes from the Legendary Liner.* Toronto: Madison Press Books, 1997.

Beauman, Fran. *The Pineapple: King of Fruits.* London: Vintage, 2006.

Beeton, Isabella. *Book of Household Management.* Lewes: Southover Press, 2003.

Blumenthal, Heston. *The Big Fat Duck Cookbook.* London: Bloomsbury, 2008.

Brears, Peter. 'Transparent Pleasures – The Story of the Jelly: Part One', in *Petits Propos Culinaires 53.* London: Prospect Books, 1996.

Brears, Peter. 'Transparent Pleasures – The Story of the Jelly: Part Two 1700–1820', in *Petits Propos Culinaires 54*. London: Prospect Books, 1996.

Brillat-Savarin, Jean. *The Physiology of Taste*. New York: Alfred A. Knopf, 1971.

Chambers, Anne. *The Practical Guide to Marbling Paper*. London: Thames and Hudson, 1992.

Cowen, Ruth. *Relish*. London: Weidenfeld & Nicolson, 2006.

Davies, Jennifer. *The Victorian Kitchen*. London: BBC Books, 1989.

Dawson, Thomas. *The Good Huswifes Jewell*. Amsterdam: Theatrum Orbis Terrarum, 1977.

Edwards, John (et al.) 'The influence of eating location on the acceptability of identically prepared foods.' *Journal of Food Quality and Preference* 14 (8) (2002): pp 647–652.

Fernandez-Armesto. *Food: a History*. London: Macmillan, 2001.

Fitzgerald, Robert. *Rowntree and the Marketing Revolution 1862–1969*. Cambridge: Cambridge University Press, 1995.

Harris, Henry G. and S.P.Borella. *All About Ices, Jellies and Creams*. London: Kegan Paul, 2002.

Henderson, Fergus. *Nose to Tail Eating*. London: Macmillan, 1999.

Horwitz and Singley, eds. *Eating Architecture*. Massachusetts: Massachusetts Institute of Technology, 2004.

Huysmans, J.K. *Against Nature*. Translated by Robert Baldick. Harmondsworth: Penguin Books, 1976.

Kelly, Ian. *Cooking For Kings: The Life of Antonin Careme the First Celebrity Chef*. London: Short Books, 2003.

Marshall, Agnes B. *Mrs. A.B. Marshall's Larger Cookery Book of Extra Recipes*. London: Marshall's School of Cookery, 1897.

McGee, Harold. *McGee on Food & Cooking: an Encyclopedia of Kitchen Science, History and Culture*. London: Hodder and Stoughton, 2004.

Plat, Hugh. *Delightes for Ladies*. London: Crosby Lockwood, 1948.

Richardson, Tim. *Sweets*. London: Bantam, 2002.

Rutherford, Jessica. *A Prince's Passion: the Life of the Royal Pavillion*. Brighton: Brighton and Hove City Council, 2003.

Shopsin, Kenny. *Eat Me: The Food and Philosophy of Kenny Shopsin*. New York. Knopf, 2008.

Steingarten, Jeffrey. *It Must've Been Something I Ate*. New York: Vintage Books, 2003.

Strong, Roy. *Feast: a History of Grand Eating*. London: Jonathan Cape, 2002.

Taillevent. *Le Viendier de Taillevent*. Translated by James Prescott. Oregon: Alfarhaugr Publishing Society, 1989.

Taillevent. *The Cookery Book*. Translated by David Atkinson. York: Michael Sessions & Colleagues, 1992.

Theodore Garrett. *The Encyclopaedia of Practical Cookery*. London: Upcott Gill, 1892.

Toulmin Smith, Lucy, ed. *Expeditions to Prussia and the Holy Land made by Henry, Earl of Derby*. London: Camden Society, 1894.

Wilson, C. Anne. *Food and Drink in Britain: from the Stone Age to Recent Times*. London: Constable, 1973.

Young, Carolin. *Apples of Gold in Settings of Silver*. New York: Simon & Schuster, 2002.

Websites: Day, Ivan. www.historicfood.com

AUTHORS' ACKNOWLEDGMENTS

There's a vast crew of people who have helped us realise the jelly dream. Parents and families who took us seriously when we turned our backs on reasonable careers to become jellymongers. They've been first to be drafted in for madcap projects, schemes, and scenarios and give the business a righteous backbone. To Abra Bompas, who put up with sticky floors when we started the business in her kitchen.

Our agent the mighty Isabel Atherton of Creative Authors who originated the concept of a jelly cookbook and has been heroic in making it reality.

Thanks to all the Anova Books people starting with our editor Emily Preece-Morrison, Polly Powell and Georgie Hewitt for hours of work and belief in this project. To photographer Chris Terry and stylist Wei Tang for making the recipes in the book look genius. To Mo Coppoletta and Hudson at New River Head, Jane and Mike at The Quality Chop House and Fontaine at Factory Studio for assistance with shoot locations. To Tamzin Ferdinando and Karl Blackwell for shoot assistance. And to Caroline Curtis and Constance Novis for editorial assistance.

To Greta Ilieva for taking the magical photograph of St. Paul's that has starred in newspapers on seven continents.

To Ivan Day, a major influence, inspiration and our food idol.

University College London and the Bartlett School of Architecture for generously lending us buildings, workshops and equipment. To Professor Stephen Gage for first encouraging us to explore the link between food and architecture through jelly, Dr Andrea Sella for opening the doors of perception and his chemistry laboratory and Dr James Kneale for the historical grounding.

A big shout out to our talented crew and co-conspirators. The indomitable Robin Fegen, who has jellied all over the world whilst writing his book *Tracksuit*: a story about pets 'n' vets. To Andrew Compton, Douglas Murphy, Nick Westby and Hugo

Richardson, a real vet. And not forgetting the scads of interns who produce the most astonishing results on ridiculously small budgets.

Elephant loads of thanks to everyone who got sucked into the process and who we've forgotten to thank here. We really are the shits you always thought we were.

To Harry's girlfriend, Cecilia Carey, for spectacular stage design. To Sam's girlfriend, illustrator Emma Rios. who gave us our first logo within a week of setting up and who forced us to get naked for her 2D banquet photograph'—another photo that has gone around the world. They help at every event; apparently it's the only way to get to see their boyfriends. We'll go on holiday next year! With love...